BOTH SIDES OF HEAVEN

"EVERYONE WHO IS CAREFUL WITH THIS BOOK ...,

HE IS LOVED BY ANGELS, ARALIM, TROOPS, SERAPHIM, CHERUBIM,

OPHANIM, AND THE THRONE OF GLORY"

FROM HEKHALOT ZUTARTI

BOTH SIDES
OF
HEAVEN

A COLLECTION OF ESSAYS EXPLORING THE ORIGINS,
HISTORY, NATURE AND MAGICAL PRACTICES OF
ANGELS, FALLEN ANGELS AND DEMONS

EDITED BY SORITA D'ESTE

PUBLISHED BY AVALONIA

Published by Avalonia

BM Avalonia
London
WC1N 3XX
England, UK

www.avaloniabooks.co.uk

BOTH SIDES OF HEAVEN
Copyright © Sorita d'Este
Individual contributors retain copyright of their essays and artwork.

ISBN-10: 1-905297-26-2
ISBN-13: 978-1-905297-26-9

First Edition, 21 June 2009
Design by Satori

Cover Image "The Fall" by Emily Carding (c) 2009

British Library Cataloguing in Publication Data. A catalogue record for
this book is available from the British Library

Cover Image "The Fall" by Emily Carding

For more information on her work see www.childofavalon.com

"There are none such nor equal unto their perfection"

THE SALKELD TREATISE ON ANGELS

ACKNOWLEDGEMENTS

This project was born out of the desire to bring together the views, experiences and research of individuals who share a passion for Angels and/or Fallen Angels in one place. Of course it would be impossible to really do such a thing comprehensively in a collection such as this, but hopefully *Both Sides of Heaven* will act as a doorway for others to continue the work in many manifest ways into the future, and inspiration for others to not simply put *'Angels'* in a category of either *'New Age'* or as part of *'unacceptable patriarchal religion'* – because they are a great deal more universal than just that. To restrict your knowledge, is to restrict your understanding and perception.

I would like to thank the following individuals who gave their time, knowledge, enthusiasm and insights to this project. Firstly the contributors – Aaron Leitch, Adele Nozedar, Charlotte Rodgers, Dan Harms, Diana Allam, Emily Carding, Jake Stratton-Kent, Julia Phillips, Katherine Sutherland, Kim Huggens, Maestro Nestor, Melissa Harrington, Michael Howard, Payam Nabarz, Rufus Harrington and Stephen Skinner. Thank you!

I would like to express a special thank you to Emily Carding who at the 11th hour stepped in and painted the highly symbolic painting "The Fall" for the cover of this book, taking a break from her work on the *Transparent Oracle* to do so, YOU are a shining and rising Star!

Finally, a big thank you to my husband and long suffering partner, David Rankine, for his contribution, patience, insights and help with the editorial work on this project, as well as his support and help with so many other things. You are my Angel.

TABLE OF CONTENTS

CONTRIBUTORS

(ALPHABETICAL BY FIRST NAME)

Aaron Leitch

Aaron Leitch has been a scholar and spiritual seeker for more than two decades. His writings cover a wide spectrum of subjects from Middle Eastern Mythology, Solomonic mysticism, Shamanism, Neoplatonism to Hermeticism, Alchemy, Traditional Wicca, Neopaganism, Ceremonial Magic, Angelology, Qabalah, Enochiana through to African Diaspora Religions, Psychology and Modern Social Commentary. He is the author of *Secrets of the Magickal Grimoires*, and a forthcoming *Encyclopedic Lexicon of Dr. John Dee's Angelical Language*. For more info see: www.myspace.com/aaronleitch or kheph777.tripod.com

Adele Nozedar

Adele Nozedar is the author of *The Secret Language of Birds* and *The Element Encyclopedia of Secret Signs and Symbols*. She lives in a wilderness part of Wales with husband Adam Fuest, where they run Twin Peaks Studios. Adele also owns Nepal Bazaar and Spellbound, in Hay on Wye. She is currently engaged in researching and writing a hard-hitting, non-fluffy book about Angels.

Charlotte Rodgers

Charlotte Rodgers is a N.D.M.P (non-denominational magickal practitioner) artist and writer who lives a quiet life in Somerset dealing with the consequences of experimental creative, magickal work.

Dan Harms

Dan Harms is the author of the *Cthulhu Mythos Encyclopedia* and co-author of *The Necronomicon Files*. He obtained a masters in anthropology from the University at Buffalo and a masters in library and information science from the University of Pittsburgh. He currently works as a librarian in upstate New York. His hobbies include reading, role-playing games, and listening to the stories people make up about his beliefs and motivations. See http://danharms.wordpress.com/ for more details.

David Rankine

David Rankine is an esoteric researcher and author of more than 20 books on the subject of magic, mythology and ancient religion. These include *The Veritable Key of Solomon, The Goetia of Dr Rudd* and the *The Practical Angel Magic of Dr John Dee's Enochian Tables* (co-authored with Stephen Skinner) and *Practical Planetary Magick, Climbing the Tree of Life* and *The Isles of the Many Gods*. He has been studying, practicing and researching the Qabalah, Ceremonial Magic and the Occult since the 1970's. He lives in Wales with his wife Sorita d'Este and son. Visit his website at www.ritualmagick.co.uk

Diana Allam

Diana is an Alexandrian High Priestess, and was first initiated in 1984; in the early 1990's she joined the magical lodge *Companions of the Rainbow Bridge*. She was trained by Rufus Harrington & Julia Phillips in a Magical system known as *Hermetics*, which she now teaches to others. As a Magician she has developed a deep relationship with the Angelic Realm, and is currently studying Madeline Montalban's Angelic course run by Jo Sheridan & Alfred Douglas of the Order of the Morning Star, she can't swim but does have two 'O' levels.

Emily Carding

Emily Carding is a self-taught artist and author, as well as a Priestess, lyricist, actress, singer and mother. As a visionary artist her work is sourced from the truth and beauty of the inner realms, mythology and the reality of magick. She is the creatrix of the groundbreaking and completely original *Transparent Tarot* which is designed to be read in layers. Her *Tarot of the Sidhe* which was published as a collector's majors only deck by Adam McLean in 2006 will be available in its complete form from 2011. She is currently working on a circular transparent oracle deck inspired by the seven directions and the intricate interconnectivity of the universe and the otherworld, which will be available from Schiffer Books in 2010. Visit her website at www.childofavalon.com

Jake Stratton-Kent

Jake Stratton-Kent is editor of *The Equinox-British Journal of Thelema*. He describes himself as an *'unaligned pagan Thelemite'*. His work has chiefly involved the promulgation and development of *English Qaballa* as a magical system. A practical magician for nearly four decades, his focus is the grimoires and the Hellenic world. Scarlet Imprint recently published his reconstructed and extensively commented edition of the *Grimorium Verum* under the title *The True Grimoire* (volume one of his *Encyclopaedia Goetica*). He is currently working on Volume Two, an extensive survey of the Greek origins and mythic background of goetia, with its roots in chthonic religion and the magical papyri; showing that properly understood goetia is the only continuous tradition in modern neo-paganism.

Julia Phillips

Julia Phillips has been studying esoteric subjects since 1971, initially at the Society of Psychical Research in London. By the 1980s her interest in tarot and hermetic magic encouraged her to specialise and she began to teach both subjects in the mid 1980s. She is the author of *The Witches of Oz* (Capall Bann, 1994), a guide to the practice of Wicca in the southern hemisphere, and contributed to *Practising the Witch's Craft* edited by Douglas Ezzy (Allen & Unwin, 2003), *Bast and Sekhmet: Eyes of Ra* by Storm Constantine & Eloise Coquio (Hale, 1999); *The Encyclopedia of Modern Witchcraft and Neo-Paganism* by Shelley Rabinovitch & James Lewis (Citadel Press, 2002); and *POP! Goes the Witch* edited by Fiona Horne (Disinformation Company Ltd, 2004). For the last two years Julia has been researching the life of occultist Madeline Montalban for a biography to be published by Neptune Press.

Katherine Sutherland

Katherine Sutherland is an occult scholar and practitioner with wide ranging interests. She is interested in the Renaissance and Early Modern period and the effects of historic workings on modern practices. Also a poet and author of fiction, Katherine is currently working on a children's novel focused on a character not dissimilar to Dr John Dee. Her poetic reworking of the Persephone myth entitled *Underworld* is currently awaiting publication and will be available in 2009. Katherine is a Priestess in the Fellowship of Isis, and a devotee of the divine path that her gods have chosen for her.

Kim Huggens

Kim Huggens is a Pagan Tarot reader and PhD student in the Ancient History Department of Cardiff University. She is the co-creator of *Sol Invictus: The God Tarot* (Schiffer Books, 2008) and the forthcoming *Pistis Sophia: The Goddess Tarot*. She has had recent work published in *Horns of Power*, and *Priestesses, Pythonesses, Sibyls* edited by Sorita D'Este, and is the Editor of online Pagan magazine *Offerings*. When not getting orgasmic about ancient voodoo dolls and Sumerian cunieform writing, she works in a vetinary clinic, plays Dungeons and Dragons, and practices Vodou.

Maestro Nestor

Maestro Nestor's interest in the occult stemmed from an interest in the darker aspects of magic during his teens, including Satanism which he practiced until his early twenties. On a trip to New York things changed when during a book buying spree he encountered Cavendish's *The Black Arts* and Waite's *The Book of Black Magic* which introduced him to the grimoire traditions, and since then he has explored the *right hand path* traditions extensively. His work has previously been published on a variety of websites, as well as in Swedish language magazines. He is currently working on a series of books on the practice of grimoire magic. Find out more about his work by visiting www.grimoiremagic.com

Melissa Harrington

Melissa Harrington is a Wiccan High Priestess who played a key role in the revival of the OTO in Britain in the mid 1990's, while managing London Pagan Federation. She has since retired from such public organisations to enjoy raising her young family in the countryside of Cumbria, and her personal focus is on a gentle connection to the seasons, to Nature and to the deep beat of the earth's heart. Melissa was awarded a Ph.D for her research on men and Wicca, and continues with her academic writing. She is particularly interested in the psychodynamics of ritual and the technology of magic. For the last twenty years she has been experimenting with creating innovative rituals for groups of two to two hundred people of various paths, in various countries, that aim to achieve gnosis, ecstasy and enlightenment via techniques as varied as meditation and fire-walking.

Michael Howard

Michael Howard is a writer, researcher, editor and publisher. Since 1976 he has been the editor and publisher of *The Cauldron* witchcraft magazine. (www.the-cauldron.org.uk) He has written extensively, and his books include *The Book of*

Fallen Angels, and *The Pillars of Tubal Cain* (with Nigel Jackson). In the 1960s he was a member of the Luciferian Order of the Morning Star and was also initiated into the three degrees of modern Gardnerian Wicca. Today he is an empowered initiate of the traditional witchcraft sodality known in the outer as the Cultus Sabbati, founded by the late Andrew Chumbley. He can be contacted by post at BM Cauldron, London WC1N 3XX, UK or by e-mail: mike@the-cauldron.fsnet.co.uk

Payam Nabarz

Persian born Payam Nabarz is a Sufi and a practicing Dervish. He is a Druid in the Order of Bards, Ovates and Druids, and a co-founder of its *'Nemeton of the Stars'* Grove. Magi Nabarz is a revivalist of the Temple of Mithras, and is working toward becoming a Hierophant in the Fellowship of Isis. He was the founder of Spirit of Peace, a charitable organisation dedicated to personal inner peace and world peace via interfaith dialogue between different spiritual paths. His work has been published in numerous esoteric magazines including *Pagan Dawn*, *Touchstone*, *Stone Circle*, *The Little Red Book*, *Pentacle*, *White Dragon*, *Silver Star*, *The Cauldron*, *Fezana* and the *Sufi*. He is the author of *The Mysteries of Mithras*, *The Persian 'Mar Nameh'*, and *Stellar Magic*. For more information on his work see www.stellarmagic.co.uk or www.myspace.com/nabarz

Rufus Harrington

Rufus Harrington is a Wiccan High Priest and initiate of the Western Mysteries who has spent many years studying Elizabethan magic. He has reconstructed the rituals of that era's most famous magician, John Dee, using Dee's original diaries, and related documents. Rufus is particularly interested in Enochia, the revival of Pagan religion, and the eternal truth of the path of initiation, and is the founder of the Enochian Magical Order, The Temple of Flame. Rufus works as a Consultant Cognitive Behavioural Psychotherapist, with practices in London and the North of England, and is an ex-Vice President of the Pagan Federation.

Stephen Skinner

Stephen Skinner is widely credited with introducing Feng Shui to the west, producing the first book on the subject in English in 1976, *Living Earth Manual of Feng Shui*. With Francis King he co-produced many well loved books including *Techniques of High Magic* and *Nostradamus*. He was the driving force behind Askin Publishers, producing classic works by authors such as John Dee, Cornelius Agrippa, Paracelsus, Aleister Crowley and Austin Osman Spare, and also reawakening interest in Enochian magic through his publications. With David Rankine he has co-authored the *Sourceworks of Ceremonial Magic* series, including *The Veritable Key of Solomon*. For more information on Stephen's work see his website www.sskinner.com

Sorita d'Este

Author and esoteric researcher Sorita d'Este describes herself as a student of life's little mysteries. She is passionate about the western esoteric traditions of magic and mysticism. Her interests in a wide range of world pantheons, including Celtic, Egyptian and Greek, as well as the grimoires, witchcraft and ceremonial magic; are reflected in her published work. Previous to *Both Sides of Heaven*, she has edited three other anthologies for Avalonia: *Priestesses, Pythonesses & Sibyls*; *Horns of Power* and *Hekate Keys to the Crossroads*. She is the author of more than a dozen books, including *Hekate Liminal Rites*, *The Visions of the Cailleach*, *Wicca Magickal Beginnings*, *Practical Elemental Magick*, *Practical Planetary Magick* and *The Isles of the Many Gods*. Visit her website & blog at www.sorita.co.uk for more information on her work.

WINGED ANGEL WITH SCYTHE AND HOURGLASS,
OF DORE ABBEY, HEREFORDSHIRE (ENGLAND)

INTRODUCTION

A Host of Winged Messengers

By Sorita d'Este

Heaven is by its very nature above us, the infinite expanse of the stars and the void. In contrast the underworld is below us, under the earth. For thousands of years the interplay of heaven and earth has defined human spirituality and myths, shaping views of the denizens of the different realms. Beings who dwell in the heavens have commonly been portrayed as being winged, indicating their ability to fly across the heavens, a quality envied by man since he first saw birds flying.

One of the great magical axioms, recorded on the Emerald Tablet of the magician god Hermes, is *'As above, so below'*. This phrase emphasises the interconnectedness of the different realms, and makes us realise that we can create our own heaven, mirroring the divine realm perceived above by realising our own inner divinity and manifesting it below, here on the Earth. This was expressed perfectly in the Orphic Oath of the ancient Greek mysteries, where the initiate declared *"I am a child of earth and starry heaven."*

Heaven was often formed from the body of a goddess or god, either living, such as the Egyptian stellar goddess Nuit, and the Greek goddess of the night sky Nox, or dead and used to create the universe, like the Sumerian goddess Tiamat. After being killed by the god Marduk, Tiamat's body was dismembered and used to form the earth and the heavens. Thus the god Marduk *"opened doors on both sides of heaven, and strengthened the doors on the left and the right."*[1]

The Origins of Angel

The word *Angel* comes from the Greek word *angelos* meaning *'messenger'*, which evokes images of beautiful winged figures, though it *"is a name of their office and not of their nature"*.[2] Winged guardian spirits may be found as far back as ancient Sumeria c.3000 BCE. These guardians were both winged humans and winged animals, like lions or bulls. Subsequent religions would all include spiritual creatures depicted as winged human figures.

Considering the meaning of the word angel, the divine messages delivered by angels through the ages have been many and significant. Gabriel, who was originally associated with fire, is the greatest of the messengers. He indicated the coming of the messiah to Daniel, he visited Zachary and told him his son would be named John (the Baptist), and he told Mary she was pregnant with Jesus. Gabriel also delivered the Qur'an to Mohammed, founding Islam. Michael too played his role as a messenger, speaking to Moses from the burning bush and delivering the magical demon-binding ring to Solomon (as described in the second century CE proto-grimoire, the *Testament of Solomon*). Gabriel (Jibril) and Michael are two of the four main angels in Islam, together with Raphael (Israfel) and Azrael (Malak al-Maut). These are all examples from what are sometimes collectively known as the Abrahamic religions.

As empires fell and rose, so too did religions, and where once the Sumerian gods and spirits reigned, came the religion of Zoroastrianism. The Ahuras (angels) and Daevas (demons) of this Persian religion are explored in depth by Payam Nabarz in

---

1 Near Eastern Religious Texts Relating to the Old Testament, Beyerlin, 1978.
2 Treatise of Angels (Sloane MS 2594, John Salkeld, 17th century.

his essay *Zoroastrian Angels and Demons*. In ancient Greece too, daimones were often depicted as winged human figures, and the nature of these beings is discussed by Kim Huggens in her essay *Between Gods and Men*.

As well as angels, a number of ancient gods and goddesses were frequently shown with wings, such as the Egyptian goddesses Isis and Maat, the Greek Anemoi (wind gods) and the goddesses Iris and Nike, the Mithraic god Aion and the Sumerian goddess Lilith. Of course the god or goddess of one religion might become the demon of another, and *Loving Lilith* by Melissa Harrington explores the different views that have developed of this complex figure, alternately viewed as goddess, demon and free-willed first created woman.

The idea of messengers having wings is not limited to angels, as can be seen by the Greek winged messenger goddess Iris, and the god Hermes, depicted with wings on his sandals and helmet rather than attached to his body though. Likewise the Thunderbird of Native American tales, was a giant bird, and used his wings to good effect, to cause storms or to carry messages from one spirit to another.

The Nature of Angels

The frequent occurrence of winged goddesses raises the issue of whether angels should be depicted as male, female or both. Whilst the tendency has become for angels to always be portrayed as masculine, or occasionally feminine but still male, this was not always the case. Dr Thomas Rudd, arguing against the German scholar Abbot Johannes Trithemius' insistence that angels were male, declared:

> *"And if Trithemius or any other natural philosopher, doth but seriously & well observe, they shall find that true wisdom is always painted in a woman's garment."*[3]

---

3 Janua Magica Reserata (Harley MS 6482), Thomas Rudd, mid-17th century.

A common perception in Renaissance magical texts was recorded in the *Salkeld Treatise of Angels*, which viewed them as existing to each fulfil specific functions. It stated:

> *"First they be no Gods but most perfect Creatures produced by the omnipotent hand of God for that unity simplicity and independence be most perfect attribute."*[4]

When the nature of angels was considered, so too the consideration of their constitution was raised, i.e. what are the bodies of angels made of? Angels were generally perceived as being made of the purest and rarefied part of the Air, hence their ethereal nature. However when some of the angels fell, it was believed that the Air became thicker as they came closer to Earth, giving them somewhat more substantial bodies, able to take on a more solid physical form, and also suffer pain more easily in punishment for their actions.

This thickness of air in the body of fallen angels (and also demons) is one of the reasons why the grimoires directed the magician to wield a sword, as this could cleave through the body of the spiritual creature and cause it pain. Effectively it meant the sword was a magical weapon, blessed by God (hence the divine names engraved on the blade), and a means of defence for the magician from any attacks. It is also interesting to note in this context that angels were often depicted bearing swords, and this may be one of the reasons for this.

Not all angels were said to be formed of Air, an exception to this being the Order of Angels called the Seraphim (*'fiery ones'*), whose bodies were said to be made of the highest form of fire (arguably light). Many of the most significant of the well-known angels, from both sides of heaven, were said to be of the Seraphim, such as Lucifer, Michael, Gabriel and Uriel. In Islam too, the Djinn are said to be beings of fire. The highest of the three orders of Djinn are described as winged humans, and like

---

4 Treatise of Angels (Sloane MS 2594, John Salkeld, 17th century.

humans Djinn have free will and roam the earth, making them more akin to fallen angels than angels.

Fallen Angels

"Non Serviam - I will not serve!"

Are the words popularly attributed to the archangel Lucifer, greatest of the angels, at the time of the first fall. According to popular perception, when Lucifer demonstrated what is called pride by some and free will by others, he caused the first divine conflict, resulting in his ejection from heaven with an unspecified number of angelic supporters. This figure is popularly one third, being drawn from a line in *Revelations 12:4* which is not specifically about angels: *"And his tail drew the third part of the stars of heaven, and did cast them to the earth."*

This figure did however turn up as a result in John Milton's *Paradise Lost*, when he equated the angels to stars and wrote:

> *"Art thou that traitor angel ... Who ... in proud rebellious arms, drew after him the third part of Heaven's Sons?"[5]*

Likewise the actual fall referred to in the Bible, is in the New Testament in *Revelations 12:7-9*, and makes no mention of Lucifer:

> *"And there was war in heaven: Michael and his angels fought against the dragon; and the dragon fought and his angels, And prevailed not; neither was their place found any more in heaven. And the great dragon was cast out, that old serpent, called the Devil, and Satan, which deceiveth the whole world: he was cast out into the earth, and his angels were cast out with him."*

Significantly this fall is prophesied as a future event, not a past one, a fact which is startling when the implications are realised. Not only does this negate many of the ideas about the Fall as being invalid due to it not having happened in the Bible

---

5 Paradise Lost II.689-92, Milton, 1667.

and thus being assumption and speculation, but it also suggests that the place of the dragon and his angels is in heaven until the fall at the end of days, not in any hell!

The second fall, which occurs earlier in the Bible (and is actually the only past fall mentioned), implied in *Genesis*, was the result of desire. This could again be argued as free will to follow desire rather than the divine plan, as is clear from the more specific details given in the apocryphal Book *1 Enoch*. Expanding on the reference in *Genesis 6:4*, *1 Enoch* lists the main leaders of the second fall, as well as the various *'gifts'* they gave to mankind, such as astrology, cosmetics, jewellery, metalworking, root magic and sorcery.

The nature and significance of these fallen angels is discussed by Rufus Harrington in *Fallen Angels and Legends of the Fall*, and by Michael Howard in *The Myth of the Fallen Ones*. Diana Allam gives a personal account of her dealings with fallen angels in *Azazel & Shemyaza, Sex, Drugs & Rock 'n' Roll*. Demonstrating how fallen angels have influenced the development of magic, David Rankine explores *The Fallen Angels and the Goetia*, and Julia Phillips shares insights into *Madeline Montalban, Elemental and Fallen Angels*.

Over the centuries it has been suggested that faeries are a type of fallen angel, being *"too bad for heaven and too good for hell!"* The links between angels and fairies are the theme of *The Salvation of the Sidhe* by Emily Carding.

Lucifer

Lucifer is frequently described as the greatest of the fallen angels, begging the question, who was Lucifer? The early Church fathers like Origen and Eusebius equated him to the Satan of *Revelations*, a questionable piece of theology which set the tone for centuries of misunderstandings and has effectively buried his origins. From the eleventh to thirteenth centuries, the Cathars used the name Lucibel to describe him as the evil Rex Mundi (*'king of the world'*), ruling the material world as God ruled the spiritual one, and re-emphasising the dualistic division of above and below. This name, Lucibel, would surface in the French witch trials of the Middle Ages as a name for the devil, adding to the misdirection and propaganda.

In the late nineteenth century work *Aradia: Gospel of the Witches* (1899) by the American anthropologist Charles Leland, a very different of Lucifer was presented as worshipped by Italian witches:

> *"Diana greatly loved her brother Lucifer, the god of the Sun and of the Moon, the god of Light, who was so proud of his beauty, and who for his pride was driven from Paradise. Diana had by, her brother a daughter, to whom they gave the name of Aradia."*[6]

In more recent times the magician Madeline Montalban (discussed by Julia Phillips in her essay) used the name Lumiel (*'light of god'*) to describe Lucifer. Considering the role of Lumiel in the Merkavah tradition of Qabalah, this is an interesting choice. Lumiel is the angel who has the secret which allows the Merkavah rider to ascend to the seventh heaven unchallenged, and indeed bears the seal which allows the rider to pass through all of the heavens unchallenged. Clearly this is an immensely powerful role, as it means he is the only angel who can take a person straight into the presence of God, who dwells on the throne in the seventh heaven.

It has been suggested that his name (*'light-bearer'*) was a Latin form of the Hebrew angel Uriel, the *"light of god"*. Although this might seem paradoxical with Uriel being the angel of salvation, he was also described as the bearer of the keys of hell, which would be appropriate for the chief fallen angel. However Lucifer was used as a Latinized form of the Greek name for Venus as the morning star, Phosphorus. Significantly, the light-bearer (*Phosphorus*) who was also the key-bearer (*Kleidouchos*) was the goddess Hekate.

---

6 Aradia: or the Gospel of the Witches, Leland, 1899.

The LightBearers

Hekate not only shared the title of *Phosphorus* with the virgin goddess Artemis, both were also given the title of *Angel* at times. In the case of Hekate she was ruler of both angels and daimons.

By the time of the *Chaldean Oracles* in the second century CE, there was a hierarchy of orders of angels serving under the goddess Hekate, these being *Iynges* (*Wrynecks*, after the bird), the *Synocheis* (*Connecters*) and the *Teletarchai* (*Rulers of Initiation*). This triad was probably one of the inspirations for the three triads of angelic orders which formed the hierarchy in the *Celestial Hierarchy* of Pseudo-Dionysius the Areopagite in the early sixth century CE. This contributed to the foundation for the structure of angelic hierarchies used in the subsequent Christian orthodoxy and the grimoires.

The Hierarchies of Angels & Demons

Where the angels, particularly the archangels who rule the angelic orders, do stand apart from their fallen brethren is in their absolutely focused approach, which is task-driven by the roles they fulfil. This is described in the seventeenth century grimoire, *Janua Magica Reserata*, which observed:

> "*There is no part of the world, destitute of the proper assistance, care, keeping or attendance of the Celestial Angels, & they send down their influences through the Celestial spheres, & planets, to the place or persons sublunary, & do especially operate, according to their several & Respective Regulations.*"[7]

The major archangels are divided in a number of ways, but one of the most significant divisions is the seven who stand in the presence of God. These are Metatron, Raziel, Kamael, Michael, Gabriel, Raphael and Uriel. The latter four are commonly attributed in contemporary magic to the four elements of Fire, Water, Air and Earth, as well as having

---

7 Janua Magica Reserata, Thomas Rudd, mid-17th century.

planetary attributions, as does Kamael (also known as Samael). The planetary archangels are also considered to rule over the planetary intelligences and planetary spirits (who are also known as the planetary angels and planetary demons) as well as their orders of angels.

THE ARCHANGEL MICHAEL TRAMPLING THE DEVIL UNDERFOOT, BY USHAKOV, 1676

The ideas of the nine orders or choirs of angels can be traced back to pre-Christian times. Looking at the philosophers of ancient Greece, we can see the roots of these concepts in Aristotle's *'Intelligences'*, developing through neo-Platonists like Porphyry and his pupil Iamblichus of Chalcis (c.245–c.325 CE), who wrote the significant text *On the Mysteries of the Egyptians, Chaldeans, and Assyrians*. This was commented on by Proclus (c.410-485 CE), in his *De Magica* and *Elements of Theology*. His work was used and expanded upon by Pseudo-Dionysius the Areopagite (c.500 CE) in his *Celestial Hierarchy,* which dealt with the angelic hierarchies in great detail, and established that there were Nine Hierarchies. In the ninth century CE, the Irishman John Scotus Erigena translated the *Celestial Hierarchy* and commented on in his work *De Divisione Naturae.* From this source, fed from centuries of development, the hierarchy of angels entered the theology taught at the new centres of learning, universities, becoming incorporated into the theology, literature and grimoires, with a hierarchy of demons to match.

Heaven	Planet	Archangel	Order of Angels	Intelligence
		Metatron	Seraphim	
	Zodiac	Raziel	Cherubim	
7	Saturn	Zaphkiel	Thrones	Agiel
6	Jupiter	Zadkiel	Dominations	Jophiel
5	Mars	Kamael	Potestates	Graphiel
4	Sun	Michael	Virtues	Nakhiel
3	Venus	Uriel/ Anael	Principalities	Hagiel
2	Mercury	Raphael	Archangels	Tiriel
1	Moon	Gabriel	Angels	Malka

The attributions of archangels over the centuries was not set in stone, as can be seen by the variety of associations in different texts and traditions. However, the influence of these angels is seen particularly in the last few hundred years, in the grimoires, Qabalah, and ceremonial magic traditions. And so too, on the other side of the mirror (or perhaps heaven), are the fallen angels and demons, in a reflection of their angelic brethren. Both sides were called upon to learn wisdom, the latter perhaps to hear the side that would otherwise be censored!

Archangel	Order of Angels	Place-ment	Order of Demons	Prince
Metatron	Seraphim	1	False Gods	Beelzebub
Raziel	Cherubim	2	Lying Spirits	Pytho
Zaphkiel	Thrones	3	Vessels of Iniquity	Belial
Zadkiel	Dominations	4	Harbringers of Wickedness	Asmodeus
Kamael	Potestates	5	Deluders	Sathan
Michael	Virtues	6	Aerial Powers	Meririm
Uriel/Anael	Principalities	7	Furies	Abaddon
Raphael	Archangels	8	Accusers	Astaroth
Gabriel	Angels	9	Tempters	Mammon

An instance of archangels delivering divine wisdom was seen in the experiments conducted by Dr John Dee with Edward Kelley, resulting in the Enochian system of magic. This is considered by Aaron Leitch in The "Enochians": The True Identity of the Angels of Dr John Dee, and Katherine Sutherland in On the Wings of Rebirth: The Angels of the Renaissance World and Dee in Context.

Indeed, from the thirteenth century angel book Liber Juratus to the Key of Solomon to the French black magic grimoires of the eighteenth and nineteenth century like the Grimorium Verum, the grimoires are full of conjurations of archangels, angels, fallen angels and demons, either for gaining wisdom, or to discover treasure or manipulate events or people (the latter more through the fallen angels and demons!). A classic example of treasure hunting with spiritual creatures is presented in The Green Butterfly, Treasure-Hunting Animals, Astaroth, and King Solomon in Hiding by Dan Harms.

Abbot Johannes Trithemius wrote in 1508 in his *De Septem Secundeis* (*'Seven Secondary Causes'*) that seven archangels ruled over history in a cycle. Each angel rules for a period of three hundred and fifty-four years and four months, and we are currently in the age of Raphael, the Mercurial archangel. Considering the developments in technology and communication, he has certainly been an active archangel! The sequence of angels which goes round in cycles is:

Sequence	Angel	Planet
1	Orifiel	Saturn
2	Anael	Venus
3	Zachariel	Jupiter
4	Raphael	Mercury
5	Samuel (Samael/Kamael)	Mars
6	Gabriel	Moon
7	Michael	Sun

The orders of angels all have functions, which are often neglected by people who will call on the archangels and assume they will get a response. However as the orders of angels contain vast numbers of angels, they are an obvious place to call for angelic assistance when required, which is why conjurations to archangels usually asked the specified spiritual creature to send a substitute if they were busy. The same principle was true for demons, with spirits from lower down the hierarchy being requested if the higher demons were otherwise occupied.

Order of Angels	Planet	Function
Thrones	Saturn	Making difficult choices and judgements
Dominations	Jupiter	Focusing the will, resisting temptations
Potestates	Mars	Protection from negative emotions or creatures, overcoming passions
Virtues	Sun	Strengthen courage, humility, patience, will, coping with adversity and trauma
Principalities	Venus	Improving personal situation, handling power
Archangels	Mercury	Strengthen devotion, intuition, mind, precognition
Angels	Moon	Dealing with immediate problems, sustenance through troubles

Angels & Demons

At this point a relevant consideration is the contrast between the terms demon and angel. Demon comes from *daimon*, which means *'intelligence'* or *'individual destiny'*, whereas angel means messenger. Originally daimones were always perceived as being positive entities. The Greek philosopher Plato introduced the division between *kakodaemons* and *eudaemons*, or benevolent and malevolent daimons, in the fourth century BCE. Seven centuries later in the third century CE, the Neo-Platonic philosopher Porphyry made an interesting distinction, this being essentially that the good daimones were the ones who governed their emotions and being, whereas bad daimones were governed by them. His contemporary, Iamblichus, argued that daimons had a more ambivalent role, being essential to *"oversee nature and the binding of souls into bodies"*, and being required as part of the Theurgic process of realising the divine within.

The Byzantine historian and philosopher Michael Psellus writing on daimons in the eleventh century took the view that they were either old gods and spirits or fallen angels. He quoted various classical writers such as Homer and Hesiod, who described daimons as gods or men who underwent apotheosis. As a Christian scholar, he seemed to prefer a view that fitted into that system, and one of the quotes he used is particularly relevant, *Matthew 25:41*, which reads, *"Depart from me, ye cursed, into everlasting fire, prepared for the devil and his angels."* This Gospel acknowledges that if the view is being taken that the demons are in an infernal hierarchy, they are in fact fallen angels. Considering the names of demons, it is then clear that some of the demons, or fallen angels, were derived from old gods, such as Astoreth (Astarte), Baal (Belial) and Horus (Haures), or straight assimilations such as the gods Pluto and Serapis, and others were mythological creatures, such as the Phoenix (Phenix), Pytho (Python) and Cerberus (Cerberus or Narberus).

Psellus categorised daimons in six orders, these being stellar, airy, earthy, watery, fiery and subterranean. This number increased to nine by the renaissance, so there were an equal number of demon orders in opposition to the angelic orders. However from the point of view of the grimoire tradition, as soon as we start looking at grimoires like the *Goetia*, it becomes clear that the demons are generally fallen angels. Thus the messenger has become an intelligence, or to put it another way, the significant difference between an angel and a demon is that the demon has gained free will. This makes them far more akin to mankind, and far more prone to our virtues and vices too. However it could be argued, as indicated by a number of the grimoires, that a price paid for freedom is servitude, in that the fallen angels and demons may be constrained by the angelic powers. The use of angels to control demons is discussed by Stephen Skinner in his essay *Thwarting Angels*, where he demonstrates the range of occurrences of this practice, from the ancient world through to the Renaissance.

> *"And besides you must understand that the Devils may be forced and constrained by the good Angels, and this is because of the Grace which the one lost, and the other as yet retains."*[8]

Some of the most famous tales of the Renaissance were moral tales warning of the danger of dealing with demons, such as Faust and his pact with the demon Mephistopheles. Maestro Nestor gives us an account of the pitfalls that can arise if you try to follow this hazardous route in *Demons & Devils*. An entirely different approach to Goetic demons is presented by Jake Stratton-Kent in *Grimoires for Pagans*, which moves beyond the familiar, as does Charlotte Rodgers in her essay *The Face in the Mirror: A Quest for Knowledge and Conversation with the Holy Guardian Angel*. As you will see from the pages contained herein, the world of angels and fallen angels is full of surprises, and nowhere is this illustrated better than by Adele Nozedar's essay *Thirteen Unicycles in the Woods*.

Finally, when considering angels and fallen angels and demons, it is worth remembering the saying that a person is known by the company they keep. This principle may be applied to your spiritual life as much as your mundane social life, so from that perspective, consider the words of Woodbury Fernald, who wrote:

> *"It is not by particular influx, as from one or more angels, that the will of man is always swayed, but by general influx of the whole society of spiritual beings with which the man is in association, and the power on both sides, of heaven and of hell, by which he is also in equilibrium: it is thus that his will is governed, and his true and proper freedom kept intact and inviolate through the whole procedure."*[9]

---

8 Janua Magica Reserata, Thomas Rudd, mid-17th century.
9 God in his Providence, Fernald, 1859.

Bibliography

Beyerlin, Walter; *Near Eastern Religious Texts Relating to the Old Testament*; 1978; Westminster Press

Collisson, Marcus (trans); *Psellus' Dialogue on the Operation of Daemons*; 1843; James Tegg; Sydney

Milton, John; *Paradise Lost*; 2003; Penguin Classics; London

Fernald, Woodbury M.; *God in his Providence*; 1859; Otis Clapp; New York

Leland, C.G.; *Aradia or The Gospel of the Witches*; 1899; David Nutt; London

Pseudo-Dionysius; *The Mystical Theology and The Celestial Hierarchies*; 1965; Shrine of Wisdom; Surrey

Rankine, David, & d'Este, Sorita; *Practical Planetary Magick*; 2007; Avalonia; London

Salkeld, John; *Treatise of Angels*; in Sloane MS 2594; 17th century; British Library

Skinner, Stephen & Rankine, David; *The Keys to the Gateway of Magic*; 2005; Golden Hoard Press; Singapore

Taylor, Thomas; *Iamblichus On The Mysteries* (translated from the Greek); 1821; Chiswick

THE SEVEN ARCHANGELS, RUSSIAN ICON, CIRCA 1900CE

FALLEN ANGELS AND LEGENDS OF THE FALL

A rather human perspective

By Rufus Harrington

Legends of Fallen Angels, cast out by god to wreak havoc upon the Earth have always fascinated, horrified and delighted those drawn to the Occult Arts. The fallen powers are a perennial theme in Occult legend and teaching with Magicians and Witches having a tendency to identify with their charismatic, antisocial, disobedient, sexually charged imagery. The fallen powers are lionised, made into heroes and light bringers. For Occultists the Fallen ones are bringers of Wisdom. They whisper in our ears to throw off the shackles of convention, to embrace our sexuality, and make up our own minds. The Fallen Angels remind us to question authority, to challenge dogma and rebel even in the face of divine law.

Is it any wonder we rather like our fallen Angels, the archetypal bad boy rock stars of the celestial sphere, thrown down to dwell amongst us? Who would you rather bed, a local lad with his shirt hanging over his jeans, or a leather clad demon, eyes shining with starlight.

There is no doubt the fallen powers are sexy. They are powerful, disobedient, wild, champions of freedom; what's not to like?

Well Christians, and generally orthodox religions, have of course found the rebel angels to be rather a handful. Disobeying God has to be the number one sin. In fact in so many ways this goes to the heart of the matter, to obey or not to obey, that is so often the question that determines what we do with our lives. Some chose a life of obedience, while others find it much more interesting to break the rules.

Of course in reality we all need to do a bit of both. At times we are obedient to convention when this serves us well, while at other times we need to break the rules and refashion our world and define new laws. This is how we grow and develop and how the world changes. From a psychological standpoint we are all born into a world of rules and a key challenge is to internalise the rules that help us and reject those that stifle our growth. We need to learn some of the wisdom of our parents and elders but we still have to discover the world for ourselves. To do this we need some disobedience, and in this the fallen angels can perhaps become our guides.

Legends of the Fall

Legends of the fall form the bedrock of many cultures worldwide. In Christian tradition it is taught that we were created in innocence, walking with the divine in the Garden of Eden. All was pleasure and ease and there was just one rule:

> *"Don't eat the fruit of the tree of the knowledge of good and evil or you will die."*

An easy rule to keep you might think, but then again you have to take account of human nature and the power of a rather charming serpent. Eve is tempted by the serpent, who tells her that she will not die if she eats the fruit, but that her eyes will be opened and she will be as god having the knowledge of good and evil. This is just too tempting, Eve eats to become wise, despite God forbidding this, and she in her turn tempts Adam to eat of the fruit. Adam and Eve's eyes are now opened, they are no longer innocents, and are rather surprised to find themselves naked.

God of course, not famous for having a sense of humour, is not well pleased, and casts both Adam and Eve out of the

Garden. Very interestingly, if we take the James version of the Bible to have some authority, God said:

> "Behold, the man is become as one of us, to know good and evil: and now, lest he put forth his hand and take also of the tree of life, and eat, and live forever: Therefore the Lord God sent him forth from the garden of Eden, to till the ground from whence he was taken"[10]

Adam and Eve fall from grace to struggle all the days of their lives. The Garden remains forever protected by the Cherubim with flaming sword, there remaining one hope that there might be a way to return and eat from the Tree of life and thus regain eternal life.

This myth has fundamental power, as a system of belief it informs so much of the culture we take for granted. As children, so many of us were brought up in a world given meaning by this story. In some sense we were taught that we are god's creation but in some way fallen, living a life less perfect than should be, that in some way we are imperfect, sinful, lacking in grace, that perhaps we are fallen angels; but there is hope of return. If we are good, if we are obedient, then we may regain God's good favour and return to the Garden, even if it is in death, and return to heaven our true home.

In Western and Eastern traditions of magic and mysticism, these basic ideas are fundamental. In Hermetic terms we are microcosms that reflect the mystery of the Divine. For Occultists we are not only fallen angels, we are fallen gods. The way of initiation becomes a quest to restore our lost divinity to storm the gates of heaven, if need be, and eat of the tree of life. Magicians seek to awaken the secret god within, and restore the true dignity they believe to be their birth right. Cabalists seek to climb the tree of life, Wiccans walk the wheel of the year, and Buddhists seek Nirvana. We are all on journey home; we are all in some way trying to overcome our fallen state.

---

10 Genesis 4:22-3.

A psychological perspective

Psychodynamic theorists and psychologists of various traditions theorise that the sense of having fallen originates in our experience of birth. We are created in the body of woman and grow in the womb where all our needs are automatically met. Then we fall, in birth, into the human world, separated from our maternal Eden, but always remembering a heavenly place where all our needs were met. It should not be a surprise, but we now know that the baby in the womb can see and hear and remember. Any parent who has seen a placenta will know that it is made in the image of a tree, a wondrous tree of life that fed us until we were ready for birth. Is it any surprise that in so many traditions the symbolism of trees is so important? The tree of life is the first thing we see in the womb, we never forget this and psychodynamic theorists argue we yearn for this, all our lives, hoping to escape life's frustrations by returning to a blissful womb like state. If this is true, is it any wonder that legends of fallen angels so fascinate and entice us? In these legends perhaps we see echoes of our own fall. Psychologically we identify with those with whom we share similar experiences; and the fallen angels can easily become mirrors in which to see ourselves.

Angels and Fallen Angels

So what are we to make of Angels and fallen Angels? Occult teaching in various traditions insists that Angels are real. Occultists have repeatedly described in detail their experience of contact with the *'spirit world'* and Angelic forces. You only have to pick any self respecting grimoire to be confronted by a bewildering array of Angel's names, often misspelt and many unpronounceable. Not only will you find Angels, but also demons and ways to call these to do your bidding. The Fallen Angels are named, and you might say shamed, but you can't keep a good Angel down and tradition teaches how the Fallen Angels became teachers to human kind passing on God's jealously guarded secrets, for little more than a roll in the hay with daughters of Eve.

To believe in Angels is almost an article of faith for Occultists and the traditions of the teaching Angels is perhaps at the very heart of Occult tradition. The belief in unseen powers which are there to help humanity grow and progress is fundamental.

The idea of a Fallen Angel raises the question of Evil. From a philosophical perspective one man's evil is another man's good – one woman's terrorist is another's freedom fighter. It so much depends on your point of view. However, taking a more common sense perspective do we believe in unseen powers that are fundamentally dangerous and predatory to human kind?

Christians tend to believe in Fallen Angels and do believe they are predators. In chapter 12 of the *Book of Revelations* we are told of the war in Heaven between Michael and Satan:

> *"And the great dragon was cast out, that old serpent, called the Devil, and Satan, which deceiveth the whole world: he was cast out into the earth, and his angels were cast out with him"*[11]

Christian history is woven with beliefs about Satan and his fallen Angels tempting human life to follow the path of sin, the path of disobedience toward God.

Christianity, echoing old Zoroastrian tradition, tends toward a dualistic theology of good versus evil, Satan verses God. Human beings caught in the crossfire, born with free will, must chose to side with one side or the other. Occultists can, and have followed in similar systems of belief; but far from all. For many Occultists the dualistic teachings of the Christian church are exoteric nonsense; essentially a system of political control and not a means of spiritual advancement.

---

11 Revelations 12:9.

For many initiate Occultists there is no absolute divide between good and evil. The Divine is believed to indwell and perhaps transcend all of creation. There is a tendency to believe in the *'one divine power of nature'* that embraces all of life and love and death. Within this view of existence there may be predators, but this doesn't make them evil. Lions hunt and kill and eat their prey. To an Occultist this is not an act of evil; it's just nature. If you go swimming where sharks are feeding then there is a good chance you are going to get eaten. This doesn't make the shark evil; just hungry.

Bearing this view of existence in mind experience has taught me to have a certain caution with unseen powers. I met a man in Australia, where I lived for nearly two years. He was a very experienced occultist; he undoubtedly had personal problems, but had contributed in many valuable ways to the development of the magical community in Australia. When I met him he was dying and he asked me to record a record of his magical work. While spending time with him it became very clear that from a magical point of view he was in trouble. He had performed a ritual, by his own admission to show off to one of his initiates that involved summoning a particular entity described in one of the grimoires. He had performed the rite under the influence of powerful drugs and from that time forward his life had gradually fallen apart. It became more and more obvious that something was feeding off him. Quite what it was I do not know, what was certain, however, was the malign influence it cast, draining this man of his energies and twisting his personal weaknesses against him. I believe his invocation had worked. He had contacted an entity of sorts. It was certainly malign from a human point of view, but I believe he had fallen foul of a *'shark'* rather than a demon. I believe he was effectively being eaten, that in a drug fuelled state he had opened his magical aura to something that considered him food.

Personal experience

Having trained in the Occult arts from my teenage years I have had dealings with Angels and they have had dealings with me. Because of my experiences I know that other levels of intelligence, not usually seen, both exist and interact with human life. To me this is normal and not an exotic belief. The terms Angel and fallen Angel are I believe misleading, tending to conjure interesting medieval visions, but which can be rather distracting when trying to develop a better understanding of the unseen world.

When I was fifteen years old I rode my bike to the top of a hill in the town called Deal on the South coast where I lived. For the sheer fun of it I then raced down the hill, as I had many times before, the wind rushing through my hair. As I speeded down the hill; suddenly a voice spoke to me as clearly as though a person was standing next to me, *"Rufus turn left now"*. I reacted instinctively wrenching the handlebars to the left, swerving into a side road, avoiding by inches the white van that pulled out in front of me. Without the warning I would have ploughed at full speed into the side of the van and been badly injured or died. This was a simple but direct intervention in my life. Something had saved me.

In my training as a Wiccan Priest and Magician I have been taught to develop the knowledge and conversation of my own Holy Guardian Angel. A very common Occult belief is that we all evolving, perhaps from life to life, and that as we make our journey, the deeper parts of the soul migrate from life to life and body to body, that we incarnate and reincarnate. As an initiate of the mysteries I was taught methods to make me consciously aware of this part of myself. This as a practice tends to go through a number of phases, over a number of years, and reached a culmination point for myself, invoking my Holy Guardian Angel, at night on the tower top of a Welsh Castle. As I and my fellow initiates invoked, a thunder storm broke over us, lightning flashing from the heavens, and as the rain began to fall, my Angel descended. Perhaps because I am a little dyslexic, the angel was good enough to spell out its name in letters of light.

Enochian Magic, The Holy Art Gebofal

When my teachers deemed the time was right I was introduced to Enochian Angelic Magic. Famed and feared as the most powerful system of magic. The Enochia, as it has come to be known, was given by the Angels to John Dee and Edward Kelly in the sixteenth centaury. Dee recorded the visions of his seer Edward Kelly, in spiritual diaries, which survive in the British Museum manuscripts collection, where I was fortunate to study for a number of years. The Visions Dee recorded describes a system of knowledge, power and communion; opening 49 gates between human consciousness and the Divine fire of creation. The knowledge given to Dee by the Angels was described by them, as the language of creation, spoken by Adam in the Garden of Eden before the Fall.

The name Enochia derives from the diary account. The Angels describe how the knowledge they provided to Dee had previously been given by God to the Patriarch Enoch and that Enoch, with God's permission, had shared this knowledge with human kind. The Angels described how the Kings of the Earth became proud and arrogant and misused the power given to them. The Angels taught how:

> "...the Lord was vexed, and he sent in amongst them an hundred and fifty lions, and spirits of wickedness, error, and deceit: and they appeared unto them: ...and they began to counterfeit the doings of God and his power, for they had power given them to do so, so that the memory of Enoch washed away...so hath the devil delivered unto the wicked the signs and tokens of his error and hatred towards god: whereby they in using them, might consent with their fall: and so become partakers with them of their reward, which is eternal damnation..."[12]

12 A True and Faithfull Relation, Antonine Publishing, 1974, p174

Dee was taught that God sent spirits of wickedness, perhaps fallen Angels, into the world to deceive those abusing the Enochian knowledge. Dee was taught that other traditions of magic were counterfeits of the true Enochian wisdom that these falsehoods *'washed away'* the true Enochian art. The magic of opening the 49 gates between God and humankind is called in the Angelic language, *'The Holy Art Gebofal'*, and Dee is told by the Angels:

> *"Now hath it pleased god to deliver this doctrine again out of darknesse".*[13]

My introduction to the Enochia or Art Gebofal took place at Yule. The coven to which I belonged had celebrated a Wiccan circle and was feasting afterwards. Some guests had already left, while the rest remained in the darkness and candlelight of the circle. An altar dressed with candles, statues of the Moon Goddess and Horned God, was set up at the edge of the circle. By candlelight you could see the eight tools of the Witches Art. A large engraved skrying mirror was set up in the centre of the circle and I was instructed to sit in front of it. A candle in a serpent candlestick was placed close by the mirror. The High Priest opened a large magical book and began to read invocations in the Angelic language, the essence of Enochian magic.

As his words vibrated in the candlelight of the circle, an extraordinary magic began to take effect, it was as though my psyche warped in both time and space. The inner and outer worlds seemed to blend together and then the candle opened like a gateway. The normal candle flame opened, it expanded physically, witnessed by everybody in the circle; the flame, which had been an ordinary candle flame was now over a foot high. It was no longer ordinary fire, it was light and radiance, and as I looked into that light a force reached out to me, and put its mark upon me, and I knew that in some way I was one with

---

13 Ibid, 1974, p174

that force, that I always have been, and always will be. Twenty five years later I can still see that light as clearly as I did that day. It remains, burning within me, a fundamental guiding light in my life.

Making sense of these experiences

These experiences and many like them make it clear to me that life is not all it appears. I have experiences of different levels of being, existing within myself and appearing outside myself. I have experienced many times how the inner and outer reality can merge and reveal new levels of consciousness, which I think of as quite normal and very wonderful.

Making sense of these experiences is always a fascinating process and I think that very often this is where many people get themselves into trouble. We can take the sceptics path and reduce such experiences to psychological process. This is not difficult to do, there are plenty of possible psychological explanations, some of which are quite useful, but all of which are limited. On the other hand we can rely too much on Occult tradition and assume, without engaging our brains, we are in contact with Angels fallen or otherwise.

I believe we should take account of the Occult perspective and teaching. We should also not be afraid to use, Theology, psychology, modern neuroscience, cultural and social theory and anything else that might help us to make sense of these most remarkable experiences. We should also use common sense, and perhaps most importantly be willing to accept that we do not really understand these experiences. A willingness to admit we only have a partial understanding of Angels, whatever they are, lays the foundation for developing a better understanding in the future. One of the essential characteristics of mystery religions and true initiatory systems is that they do not teach truths. Instead initiates are taught how to develop their own vision and understanding. Initiates accept that any point of view is limited; and that as we expand consciousness our understanding changes. From an initiate's point of view there can be many different understandings of Angels.

A few final words

I prefer to keep things simple. I have the experience of encountering what some people call Angels or Fallen Angels, but which I prefer to call intelligences, or by the names they give me. I find it interesting and worthwhile to communicate with these intelligences and believe we are on the threshold of a much wider world. Not only are we just learning, with the help of modern science, how vast the seen universe really is; we need to also acknowledge that there is a vast unseen dimension or dimensions, interacting, with intelligence, with our own realm.

This is what I believe should be a key focus for 21st century magical practice. We should seek to build bridges and communicate better with these intelligences. To do so we need to develop our methods, and rely much less on traditions of magic fashioned in the context of dualistic Christian belief. We need to question carefully our ideas about Angels and Fallen Angels remembering we can be inspired by the 16th century without having to become prisoners of its beliefs. We need to apply common sense. Just because we make contact with something, does not mean it is necessarily wise or worth talking to. We need to be cautious; I do believe there are predators in the unseen world, as there are in all worlds. However, I have experienced beings that have saved my life and helped me in countless ways. With these intelligences I will continue to seek communion.

THE GREAT CHAIN OF BEING

DIDACUS VALADES, RHETORICA CHRISTIANA, 1579

ON THE WINGS OF REBIRTH

The Angels of the Renaissance world and Dr John Dee in context

By Katherine Sutherland

Out of the dark ages, the renaissance rose like a phoenix from the ashes of the past; and in the liminal space between the celestial and the terrestrial stands a man well known as a spy, a court philosopher, a practical scientist and an antiquarian. Dr John Dee is perhaps one of the most renowned renaissance occult thinkers; viewed either as a shadowy figure, involved in espionage and deception, a darling of the court, or a dealer with the devil. Francis Yates describes Dee as a *'renaissance magus'* who continued in England the same hermetic traditions that encompassed Ficino, Pico della Mirandola, and Giordano Bruno. Nicolas Culdee disagrees and suggests that a large part of Dee's inheritance came from Medieval sources, the writings and experiments of Roger Bacon in particular. Where Yates sees Dee as a steady exponent of European philosophy, Culdee describes as a more eclectic and empirical figure. Yet, despite disagreements, much scholarship on Dee converges on a central theme; that Dee stood on the ground where the concerns of the Renaissance age met and could not be easily distinguished.

Dee himself seems to embody the values of many times; he was in part a Medievalist, expounding the use of ancient formulae, yet also an agent in contemporary philosophy. He was an Antiquarian, concerned with the origins of Britain, and the notions of ancient cities being preserved within the earth, yet he also anticipated a scientific revolution and experimented with mechanics. He was an alchemist and astrologer who scrutinized the spiritual domain, yet as a geographer he plotted navigational charts for the physical exploration of the terrestrial world.

The alchemy and angelic realms in which Dee placed his faith are complex. He believed in a world imbued with spiritual properties, with signatures and correspondences that could reveal true nature. Each material thing was viewed as a visible home of universal power, or a congregation of powers, and the task of the enlightened one was the ability to view the constituent parts. Dee understood from the successful medicine of Paracelsus, how the stars, the fruits of the earth and the human body may constellate together to effect cure for disease. Another controversial truth which Dee understood was the concept of God within man; according to Dee, the man who understands himself may understand the universe. Dee believed he spoke with angels, both directly and via his medium, and I find it hard to disbelieve him. He was a man obsessed with learning who spent his entire life trying to resolve the mysteries of nature, and hence, achieve divine illumination. He knew too much to be affected by the malice of his contemporaries when he went beyond the bounds of established theory.

The use of a Medium allowed Dee to see beyond the confines of the physical, and through his experiences, to map the domains of a particular Renaissance spirituality. Edward Kelley, a scryer in stones, was to some a charlatan, but Dee remained faithful to him throughout their many years together. Whether looking to see what was visible in the upper air of the heavens, or buried below ground, Kelley had a handy knack of alighting on a vision which suited Dee, and thus their partnership worked well for many years. Kelley as an observer of marvels was useful to Dee as a vessel, hollow within and containing nothing, save the bright angelic airs of the heavens which his visions expressed.

The validity of Kelley's visions has long been questioned by scholars of Dee. In seeing spirits and angels appearing within the shew stone, he is documented as being open to Dee's proposition, a practice possibly similar to the auto-suggestions used by modern day mediums who are skilled in cold reading. In promoting the notion that the creatures within the stone knew not of gold, but of greater riches by far, Kelley was able to convince Dee of a world of learning through which the angelic spirits may guide him; and what could Dee do but aspire to the wisdom of the higher spiritual realm, the realm of those closest to God? His life had been consumed in pursuit of the Great Truth and apart from the common practices of mankind; nothing could now turn him from this course. Seeing rays more refulgent than gold shining within the stone, he could only continue on his journey.

Dee's obsessive nature and desire to believe in the unseen world converged as a fatal combination of qualities that lead to his eventual demise. Being a man of a certain time he held certain beliefs, and, as far as he was concerned, the angels with whom he consulted via the medium of Kelley would serve his bidding and lead him to discover great wealth and riches buried within the earth and the philosophical secrets of life itself. What ensued was a merry dance around Europe and the low countries in particular, the following of strange suggestions concerning Kelley's desire for a family and Dee being instructed to *'intermingle'* his sexual energies with Kelley's wife who had so far failed to come up with the goods. In following so called angelic instructions Dee traversed the geographic realms of contemporary European alchemy, dragging his family with him, through poverty, disease and extreme danger. Dee ended his life still believing in the angelic realm and its messengers who had appeared to visit him.

His impact as a thinker and occultist is undoubtedly enormous, although as a modern practitioner, one cannot help questioning his absolute trust in his medium who appeared to manipulate him and abandon him at will, only to appear again when he was falling on hard times or when the fancy took him. Possibly the vagaries of the angelic realm have similar nuances to the realm of men, and, maybe, one so touched as Kelley could serve as a conduit to pass on such information in a way that suited him, or perhaps, he manipulated one the greatest scholars of the Renaissance entirely for his own means and ends. It must be remembered that by even attempting such communications, Dee was treading a thin line between the accepted eccentricities and quirky behaviour allowed of a court philosopher and committing high treason. In the great chain of being, a construct said to depict the true nature of the earth and the heavens, angels serve as the messengers of god to humanity, yet the monarch or sovereign sits at the top of the chain as a representative of God on earth. Thus, by attempting to bypass the sovereign and the priesthood, Dee was dangerously close to personal revelations of a divine nature, such things being previously reserved for fervent saints and mistrusted mystics, Dee possibly damaged his credibility in documenting his angelic experiences and devalued his own work in the face of the competition. However, Dee arguably achieved immortality through his characterisation by William Shakespeare in his play *The Tempest* which centres around the magus Prospero and his relationship with airy being Ariel, who acts an angelic servitor to the main protagonist. Prospero demonstrates the power of the arts of age by first capturing her then giving her back her freedom, once she has done his bidding.

If we cast our eyes beyond Dee's intellectual training to his personal experiences it is possible to situate his conversations with angels into a broader cultural context. The angelic conversations reveal Dee's faith and understanding that his practise as a natural philosopher required him to communicate with all – the higher beings, his patrons and the public, as he believed that the day of judgement was drawing near. Dee's angel magic has tended to be minimized by scholars who prefer to stress his concrete achievements, his broad minded nature and his philosophical importance to the Elizabethan Renaissance. However, Dee's magic cannot and should not be excused away; perhaps the principal difficulty being that most commentators fail to understand it.

It should also be made clear that Dee's angel magic must be sharply distinguished from spiritualism, a practise in which those desperate for proof an afterlife implore invisible beings to make contact with them. Dee's approach sought to make man conscious of his own divinity. Dee's contribution to magic consists of a mass of raw materials, which although erratic in quality provides the cornerstone to the Enochian system. Dee communicated with a vast array of angels during his conversations, both the famous and the obscure, all of whom possessed individual personalities, demeanours and appearances. Although most angels appeared to Dee as men, some who were important to the evolution of the conversation appeared as women.

Dee's celestial beings, whether referred to as spirits, intelligences or angels were important members of the divine structure of the cosmos. The best known angels in Dee's conversations are the archangels of the Judeo-Christian tradition; Gabriel, Michael, Raphael and Uriel. Dee believed that their primary function was to serve as messengers between god, humanity and other members of the celestial hierarchy. Gabriel first occurred in conversation around 1583. As the angel of resurrection, annunciation and revelation, he was known as the guardian of the Garden of Eden and was set to remain at the gates of paradise until the restitution of the natural world; Gabriel was also regarded as the guardian of the moon by other authorities. Early modern authors were intrigued by Gabriel, possibly due to Trithemius' suggestion in *De Septem Secundeis* that the historical period ruled by Gabriel began in 1525.

The angel Michael is also prominent in Dee's spiritual conversations, his chief attributes being the scales of judgement and the sword of justice. According to Trithemius, Michael was the guardian of the sun, whilst Agrippa attributed his guardianship to quicksilver; both authors also gave him key alchemical connotations by aligning him with the planet Mercury. Dee's experience with the angel Michael can be slotted neatly into this framework; Michael appeared with his sword of justice in 1582, during which time he told Dee that he would reveal the secrets of the book of nature that had not been given to Solomon.

Raphael was also introduced into the conversations in 1582. Although he was not as frequent a communicant as Gabriel or Michael, he was the only known angel to communicate with Dee in his later life. Another angel, Uriel also had an important role in the surviving angelic conversations. He was the first angel to speak to Dee and shared many prophecies and detailed alchemical parables. During the course of these conversations, Uriel also explained the terrestrial significance of angels' revelations and acted as a problem solver when questions concerning the revelations arose.

The angel Anael appeared in the only conversation which survives from Dee's relationship with another scryer, Barnabus Saul. In this conversation Anael confessed his power over all things. Dee considered this angel to be governor of the historical period in which he lived; his opinion here differencing from received scholarly opinion.

The mighty and well known angels were not the only beings to appear in Dee's angelic conversations, there were a host of others who appear nowhere else in Christian, Jewish or Islamic systems. Although this has led some to discount them as fairies or demons, Dee considered them to be lower beings of the celestial hierarchy, more concerned with revelation and closer to man than the higher orders of angels and archangels. Angels such as Salamain, Och, and Nalvage were frequent participants in angel conversations.

Although the majority of the angels were unknown to Dee's contemporaries, the same cannot be said of Dee's immediate audience. As the divine plan for the terrestrial plane was supposed to reflect the same ordered hierarchy of the cosmos, as illuminated by the divine chain of being, the angels instructed Dee to share his revelations with the most powerful people in Early Modern Europe. Dee's conversations had never been entirely private, but as they became public, Dee was perceived as a political and spiritual threat, not only because of the content of his messages, but also due to the fact that they were delivered unmediated; without the filter of the ranks of the elite of the establishment of the church. However, in escaping from aristocratic control, Dee shared his conversations so that the worthy could fulfil God's intention and purpose, this brought Dee into direct conflict with the church in 1584. Far from suggesting fraudulence, it seemed that the Catholic establishment was concerned that Dee's activities were all too real, but questioned the nature of the spiritual communication. The institution's scepticism hinged around Dee's worldly nature, the assumption being that the man who enjoyed the earthy pleasures of married life would not provide a clean vessel through which the good of God would choose to communicate.

From 1586, Dee's angelic conversations began to become strained, under the burden of a multitude of patrons, the eyes of suspicion and the host of angels and their individual personalities. These stresses placed on Dee reveal the complex mechanics of the situation, but it is possible to suggest that Dee's unshakable faith in the power of the angelic revelations reflect his coming to terms with the practice of natural philosophy in a changing world, one which he believed was coming to an end. While working on this paradoxical situation, Dee sought a means to bridge the gap between the human world and the desire to be one with god – this being his conversations with angels.

Dee's angel conversations and their metamorphosis from the pinnacle of natural philosophy to their publication as a warning against the evils of conjuration, to suggestions that they were some form of cryptography has much to tell us about the changes which were occurring in philosophical beliefs. Dee was not regarded as delusional in his own time, however, this description emerged a century after his death, during which the effects of humanism and the reformation were being expressed in different ways; Dee's emphasis on the power of divine revelation being replaced by an emphasis on the power of human reason. As Dee's aims were shrouded in the bookishness of prophecy, alchemical parable and cabalistic allusion, it is easy to identify them as part of the allegorical past rather than an experimental and observational future. John Dee is a complex transitional figure who promoted the development of the future, but, was equally conversant with the ideas of his own time. Perhaps the key to understanding Dee is his unshakable faith in man, as a star being, capable of anything he desired. Such beliefs led Dee into the dangerous territory of angelic communication; however, by seeking universal knowledge by heavenly means, he can be regarded as a complete Renaissance man.

Primary Sources Dee's probable influences:
Agrippa, Henry Cornelius; *De Occulta philosophic libri tres*; 1533; Agrippa; Basel
(a variety of translations of Agrippa's works are widely available).
Bacon, Roger; *Friar Bacon His Discovery of the Miracles of Art, Nature and Magic. Faithfully Translated Out of Dr. Dee's Own Copy by T.M. and Never Before in English*; 1659; Simon Miller; London.
Pico della Mirandola, Giovanni; *Conclusiones Sive These DCCCC*; 1486; Romae Abbi; Publice Disputandae, Sed, Non Admissae, Introduced and annotated by Bohdan Kieszkowski, Geneva, Librarie Droz, 1973.

Trithemius, Johannes; *De Septem Secundeis*; 1508, published posthumously, Impressum Francoforti : Apud Cyriacum Iacobum, Ex Archetypo conscriptus, Anno Domini 1545

Books about Dee:

Culdee, Nicholas; *John Dee's Natural Philosophy, Between Science and Religion*; 1988; Routledge; New York.

French, Peter; *John Dee, The World of an Elizabethan Magus*; 1987; Ark Paperbacks; London

Harkness, Deborah; *John Dee's Conversations with Angels: Cabala, Alchemy and the End of Nature*; 1999; Cambridge University Press; Cambridge

Suster, Gerald; *John Dee, Essential Readings*; 1986; Aquarian Press; London

Yates, Francis; *The Occult Philosophy in the Elizabethan Age*; 1979; Routledge and Keegan Paul; London

THE FOUR AVENGING ANGELS, BY ALBRECHT DURER

THE MYTH OF THE FALLEN ONES
By Michael Howard

In *Genesis 6:4* there is a brief account of a mythic event that seems to have escaped the attention of the religious censors when the early Church councils decided what to include and what to exclude from the orthodox text of the Judeo-Christian Bible. The verse in question states:

> *"And it came to pass, when men began to multiply on the face of the earth, and daughters were born to them, that the sons of God saw the daughters of men that they were fair; and they took them wives of all which they chose...There were giants in the earth in those days; and also after that, when the sons of God came in into the daughters of men, and they bore children to them, the same became mighty men which were of old, men of renown."*

Although this account of the incarnation on Earth of the *'sons of God'* or Beni Elohim is brief, a more detailed account is given in the apocryphal *Book of Enoch* attributed to the Old Testament prophet Enoch, who *'walked with God and was not.'* It was written around 175 BCE and says that the Beni Elohim (more accurately *'the sons of the Gods'* as Elohim is plural) were in fact *'children of Heaven'* or angels who lusted after the *'beautiful and comely'* human women. The Fallen Ones or Watchers were led by a chief angel called Semjaza or Shemyaza and they descended from the heavenly realm on to Mount Hermon in modern Israel. Enoch names the fallen angels as Semjaza, Arakiba, Rameel, Kokabiel, Tamiel, Ramiel, Danel, Ezegeel, Baraqijel, Asael, Armaros, Batarael, Ananel, Zaqiel, Samsapeel, Satrael, Turel, Jonjael and Sariel.

According to Enoch, these angels took human wives and taught them *'charms and enchantments, and the cutting of roots, and made them acquainted with plants'* (herbalism and botany). Specifically Azazel (Asael) taught men how to forge swords and knives and manufacture shields and breastplates (body armour). He also *'made known to them the metals (of the earth) and the art of working them'* (mining and metallurgy). To women Azazel taught the use of antimony, *'the beautifying of the eyelids'* with kohl, and the use of precious stones and metals for decorative purposes as jewellery. Semjaza taught the art of root-cutting and enchantments; Armaros, the resolving of enchantments (magical banishing), Baraqijel, astrology; Kokabiel, the nature of the constellations (astronomy); Ezegeel, the knowledge of clouds (weather lore); Araqiel, the signs of the earth (geomancy and geology); Shamsiel, the signs of the sun; and Sariel, the course of the moon (lunar cycles and phases).

In the biblical account of the descent of the fallen angels it says that Yahweh *'saw the wickedness of men was great in the earth'*. Because he now regarded his creation as inherently evil, Yahweh decided to destroy humankind and *'wipe them from the face of the earth'* together with the birds, reptiles, mammals and fishes. However, he seems to have partly relented from the total destruction of the biosphere by choosing *'a just man'* called Noah and appointing him as the human saviour of life on Earth. It was Noah and his family who reseeded the planet after the Great Flood, a mythic event that was probably a far memory of an actual physical cataclysm in prehistoric times. Ironically, Noah's descendants also preserved the forbidden knowledge given to humankind by the Fallen Ones.

In the version of the myth given in the *Book of Enoch*, the four archangels Mikael (Michael), Raphael, Gabriel and Uriel *'looked down from Heaven and saw much blood being shed upon the earth, and all lawlessness being wrought upon the earth'*. This situation had allegedly been brought about by the actions of the Fallen Ones. They had corrupted humankind by the 'secret things' they 'disclosed and have taught their sons'. The result of the forbidden union between the incarnated Watchers and their human partners was the birth of giants, 'the mighty men of old, men of renown' described in *Genesis*, known as the Nephilim. The term 'giants' is relative and probably means they were taller than the average person of the time. These half-human, half-angelic offspring, described as 'the lawless ones', are supposed to have turned against ordinary humans and hunted them down for food. According to Enoch, they also 'began to sin against the birds and the beasts and reptiles and the fish and even began to devour one another's flesh and drink the blood'. This is why Yahweh decided to punish those humans who had cohabited with the incarnate Fallen Ones and also destroy the monstrous product of their union.

Ignoring the propaganda element in the myth of the Fallen Ones, it is pretty obvious from the description of the Watchers in The *Book of Enoch* that they acted as cultural exemplars and teachers to primitive humankind. Their activities in that role are reflected in ancient mythology worldwide where Gods are described as being born in physical form to teach the arts of civilisation to the early human race. In Jewish mythology the Beni Elohim were originally a superior order or race of angelic beings who dwelt in the highest level of Heaven and were humanoid in form. Their alternative title of 'Watchers', meaning 'ones who watch', 'those who are awake' or 'the ones who never sleep', referred to an angelic order created by God to be the earthly shepherds and teachers of humanity. Paul Huson has described the Watchers as the divine parents of the human race either as 'masters of wisdom and love' or as the 'benevolent powers of fertility and hunting' that are the witch gods and witch goddesses. It was their task to watch over and observe the evolving human race, helping and guiding it where necessary without breaking the prime directive of non-interference. Instead they ignored this divine command with unfortunate results for both themselves and their human charges.

In Jewish lore it is said that Azazel and Shemyaza, the two leaders of the Fallen Ones, had first asked Yahweh for his permission to incarnate in *'cloaks of skin'* or physical bodies and teach humanity. When the tyrant god refused their request, because he wanted to keep his human creation in ignorance, Shemyaza rebelled and led his angelic company into incarnation. Through the agency of the four archangels – Michael, Raphael, Gabriel and Uriel – who are also confusingly described as *'Watchers'* – Yahweh commanded that the fallen angels and their leaders either be bound *'under the earth'* or *'in the depths of the earth'* or destroyed completely.

In his unpublished manuscript *The Green Gospel*, the late Andrew Chumbley, past Magister of the Cultus Sabbati, stated that the spirits of the Watchers entered the hills and desolate places of the world *'to dream anew.'* They were known as the *'Mighty Ones'* or the *'Shining Ones'* and their role was to act as the guardians, guides and teachers of the human race. Other writers on the subject have suggested a link between the Watchers and the semi-divine, semi-mythical tribe of the Tuatha de Danaan or *'People of (the goddess) Dana'* who arrived in Ireland in prehistoric times. They were known popularly as the *'Shining Ones'* and according to legend descended to Earth in their ships on Beltane (May 1st) on the hill of Tara, the sacred centre of Ireland where traditionally its High Kings were crowned.

With the arrival in Ireland of Christian missionaries, the Tuatha de Danaan were downsized and downgraded into the fairy folk. They were banished into the *'hollow hills'*, just as the Watchers were bound in *'the depths of the earth'*. In *The Green Gospel* cited earlier, we have seen how the fallen angels entered the *'hollow hills'* (Elfane or the realm of Faerie). In rural communities, especially in Ireland, there has always been a persistent belief that the Fallen Ones became the faeries described in folklore and folk traditions. In his book *Demonologie* King James I described faeries as *'devils'* and the

15th century clerical authors of the infamous witch-hunting guide the *Malleus Maleficarum* or *Hammer of Witches* linked the Nephilim with the satyrs and wood sprites of classical mythology.

In the 3rd century BCE the Orthodox Christian philosopher St Origen, condemned by his peers as a heretic, claimed: *"From the beginning those who have occupied the most eminent positions among men and have been markedly superior to others have been angels in human form."* This is a reference to the survival of the half-angelic, half-human hybrid descendants of the mating between the Fallen Ones and *'the daughters of men'*. In the *Zohar* it says that although most of the Nephilim were destroyed in the Flood, their spirits proved indestructible and lived on in a disembodied state. According to Paul Huson, these spirits sometimes gain access to the material world by reincarnating in human form. He has described them as *"...intruders, ancient alien souls transmigrating from the past"*.

One of the earliest examples of the union between the angels and humans resulting in a half-angelic, half-human hybrid was the birth of Adam and Eve's eldest son Qayin or Cain. In the Bible the first woman makes the cryptic remark: *"I have gotten a man from the Lord"* (*Genesis 4:1*) in reference to her newborn son. Although it says she conceived him with Adam, the coded allusion suggests the first man was not his father. In esoteric Jewish lore Cain is the son of Eve and the serpent in the Garden of Eden myth, known as Samael or Lucifer (Lumiel or *'the Light of God'*), the first-born of the angels.

In the Bible Cain is represented as the *'first murderer'* because he killed his brother Abel in an argument over the sacrificial offerings to be made to Yahweh. Abel was a nomadic herdsmen and offered animal sacrifices to Yahweh, but Cain was a ploughman, a gardener and *'tiller of the soil'* and he offered the produce of the earth, which Yahweh rejected as unsuitable. Although Cain is depicted as the *'first murderer'* when he is exiled to the land of Nod he becomes a city builder (*Genesis 4:16-17*). In fact he named his first city after his firstborn son, Enoch. In some modern branches of the Old Craft (traditional and hereditary witchcraft) Cain is respected and revered as a cultural exemplar, the first sorcerer or magician, a master of horsemanship and the inventor of smithcraft.

In the *Zohar* it says the sons of Cain or *'children of Cain'* were known as *'the sons of God'* because his 'aspect was unlike that of the other humans'. The *Zohar* goes on to say that *'the wicked of the world'* descend from Cain and are *'half-like human beings below and half-like angels below'*. Again this is a coded reference and concerns the difference between the human intellect and the generative powers gained when early humans were expelled from the *'Garden'*. It is also a reference to the metaphysical and spiritual concept of the so-called *'witch blood'*, *'elven blood'* or *'fairy blood'*. This is the spiritual descent of the gnosis of the Watchers or Fallen Ones in the human race through successive incarnated experience. This is not a physical or genetic transmission and it has to be understood in purely spiritual terms. As Andrew Chumbley described it, in specific relationship to incarnation into the Old Craft: "*The true gnosis of the lineage [of the Children of Cain] is a secret communication as 'power' within the moment of initiation into the <u>spiritual</u> bloodline*" [my underlining for emphasis]. Chumbley used the term *'witch blood'* to make the distinction between those who were initiated, and therefore awakened into wisdom, and the non-initiated, who are still *'asleep'* and dreaming the dreams of materialism.

Nigel Jackson has said: "*The great epitome of the angelical transformation in the Western occult tradition lies in the exaltation of the psyche to its essential angelic nature, the realisation of the inner angel.*" Referring to the survival of "*the starry wisdom of the Watchers*", Paul Huson says that at the centre of traditional witchcraft is "*the cinder of the spark of that mysterious dark angelic fire which first breathed life into the clay of this world.*" In different ways they are both expressing the same truth.

Ultimately the goal of the Arte Magical is the transmutation of the human being into a *'perfected one'* and the transformation of the physical environment into a heavenly Edenic state. Encapsulated within the myth of the Fallen Ones is the esoteric teaching of the descent of spirit into matter and the alchemical transmutation of matter into spirit by its influence. As the Bruce Papyrus says: *"You shall become Gods and you shall see God in yourselves."* That is the end goal of the practice of any form of angelic magic or communion with our angelic guides and teachers, the Fallen Ones.

Bibliography and further reading:

Chumbley, Andrew; *The Green Gospel*; Unpublished
Howard, Michael; *The Book of Fallen Angels*; 2004; Capall Bann; Chieveley
Howard, Michael, & Jackson, *Nigel; The Pillars of Tubal Cain*; 2000; Capall Bann; Chieveley
Huson, Paul; *Mastering Witchcraft*; 1970; Rupert Hart-Davies

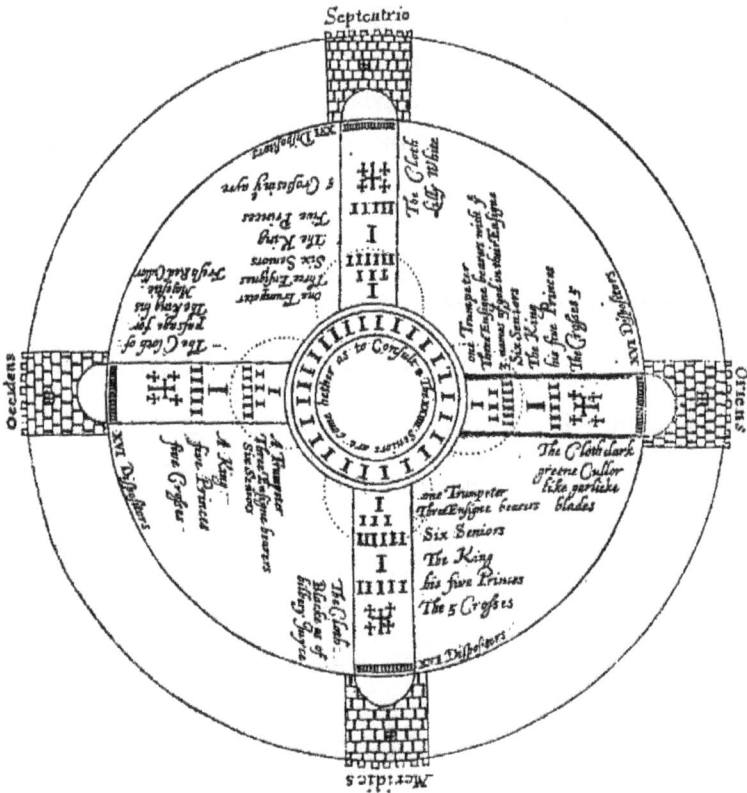

EDWARD KELLEY'S VISION OF THE WATCHTOWERS, 20TH JUNE 1584

THE "ENOCHIANS"

The True Identity of the Angels of Dr. John Dee

By Aaron Leitch

When it comes to the study of Angels - and even more so the practice of Angel Magick - no names are more inescapable than those of Dr. John Dee and Sir Edward Kelley. Not only are the journals of their practical Angelic work the most influential and often-referenced literature of its kind, but these two men have in many ways become the very archetype of the *'Wizard'* in Western culture. If that term brings to your mind white-bearded English gentlemen crouching over a crystal ball and conversing with Angelic Intelligences, it is most assuredly Dee and Kelley you are envisioning.

Dr. John Dee is perhaps most famous as court astrologer and advisor to Queen Elizabeth I. Those familiar with the history of espionage or cryptography may recognize him as *'England's first spy'* who operated for the Queen under the code *'007'* (to which author Ian Fleming nodded when he gave the same code to James Bond). Academic scholars know him best as the author of the preface to Euclid's *Elements*, a founding fellow of Trinity College and an expert on Navigation whose work made early voyages to the New World possible. Plus, of course, Dee is famous in esoteric circles as a Hermeticist, Qabalist and Angelologist.

Meanwhile, Sir Edward Kelley (who was never actually knighted as far as we know) is most famous as the medium who worked with Dee during his Angelic séances. Second to this,

Kelley is perhaps a Western archetype for the Alchemist - travelling from one court to another, promising kings and nobility that he could transform their worthless metals into gold. This was one of the most dangerous rackets one could attempt, as failure to produce as promised could quickly lead one to prison or worse. It is rumoured (but not proven) that Kelley had his ears cut off by one angry patron. It is said he met his end after falling from a prison tower, where no less a figure than the Emperor Rudolph had cast him when he failed to produce gold. Some say it was an escape plan gone awry, and others suppose it was an unofficial execution.

It is perhaps needless to say that our modern perceptions of these historic personages are not altogether accurate. They have become legendary, and their stories have been embellished over time. Of course their magickal powers have become exaggerated - such as crediting John Dee with single-handedly sinking the Spanish Armada off the coast of England in 1588. (It is suggested that he raised the storm that ravaged the fleet, while records only have him predicting the event.) However, it is just as common to find our views of these men misconstrued- rather than exaggerated- so we come to accept certain ideas about them as 'fact' when they simply are not true.

There is an understandable difficulty in separating fact from legend when discussing these two men. Historical records are thin at best, and much of what we suppose we know about them comes strictly from stories that have been passed down for hundreds of years. Fortunately, what I will cover below does not depend so much on word of mouth. Instead, I will be discussing an aspect of their lives for which we have ample record, but which has become misconstrued none-the-less: the Angelic séances themselves, and the system of magick revealed by them known as 'Enochian Magick'. Dee was an exhaustive journalist, and recorded even the minutest details of his work with Kelley. The journals extend over multiple books and hundreds upon hundreds of densely hand-written pages.

DR JOHN DEE

    I do not blame modern students for their misunderstandings of Dee's work. The information is hidden within these vast records, Dee's difficult penmanship and the same Elizabethan language we've come to dread in the works of Shakespeare and the King James Bible. Thus, students are most often left to depend on what other scholars have to say about the journals, and those scholars most often depend on the scholars before them, etc. And, to be frank, these scholars have got a lot of their information wrong.

In this essay, I hope to literally set the records straight. I want to bust the myths that abound about Enochian Magick and, especially, about the Angels from whom Dee and Kelley received the magick. By doing this, we can look at Dee's work in its proper context, and (re-)place his magickal system into the genre of Renaissance Angel Magick where it belongs. So-called *'Enochian Magick'* is most often considered an over-complicated and quite alien mystical system when compared to the Keys of Solomon and other works of classical Western Magick. Yet, when viewed in its proper context, it turns out to be quite straight-forward and rather typical of the European magick of its time.

The biggest myth I will tackle here concerns the identity of Dr. Dee's Angelic contacts. If you have done any research into the subject, you have undoubtedly encountered the assertion that Dee had discovered an entirely unique host of entities. (There is a small kernel of truth to this, but the statement is vastly misleading.) Some have even gone so far as to insist that they were not Angels at all, but where beings of a different sort who simply lied to Dee and Kelley about their true nature. Not a few students have begun to refer to them as *'The Enochians'* - dropping the term *'Angels'* entirely. And just a few, thankfully small in number, have gone so far as to suggest Dee was in contact with aliens from another planet or dimension!

To begin unravelling all of the hub-bub surrounding this subject, I'm going to set aside the identity of the Angels for just a moment, and focus instead on the very use of the term *'Enochian.'* Most often, esoteric scholars and their students assume this word specifically refers to Dee's journals and the magickal system outlined within them. This is incorrect. The word actually describes an entire genre of literature that extends many hundreds of years before the time in which Dee lived. His journals are certainly part of that genre, but they do not define it.

The Prophet Enoch is first mentioned in the Biblical *Book of Genesis* (5:21-24), where he appears in the seventh generation after Adam. He was the father of Methuselah and the great-grandfather of Noah. It is claimed that he lived an impressive 365 years, during which time he *'walked with God.'* From this passage arose apocryphal stories in which the Prophet was given several tours (either literal or visionary) of the various circles of Heaven. Then, unlike the other generational fathers listed in this chapter of Genesis, the Bible does not say Enoch died. Instead, he *'...was no more, because God took him.'* From this passage arose legends of Enoch's bodily translation into Heaven, where he was transformed by fire into the Archangel Metatron, the Voice of God.

The first apocryphal *Book of Enoch* - known as *1 Enoch* or the *Ethiopic Book of Enoch* - is supposed to have been written near 600 BCE, during the Hebrew Captivity in Babylon. Internal textual evidence suggests much Babylonian influence upon the story. Other versions were written in later generations, which draw more or less upon this original mythology. In all versions, the Prophet Enoch travels into the Heavens and is given grand tours thereof by the Archangels. One of the grandest sights he is shown is the Tablets of Heaven (aka the Book of Life), wherein all of the secrets of the universe are recorded. He is then instructed by God to copy just a small portion of these Tablets into 366 Books, and to bring them back to Earth as a gift to mankind. (It is a bit confusing, but these legendary records are called the *Tablets of Enoch* or the *Book of Enoch*, but this is not the same as the apocryphal *Book of Enoch* that contains the story!)

According to the legends, Enoch did indeed bring his Tablets back to Earth and passed them down to his descendants. Noah had them, and found the blueprints for the Ark within them. Sadly, the Tablets were lost during the Deluge itself. They were later restored unto King Solomon, who is said to have received his great wisdom from their pages. However, they were again lost when Solomon fell from grace.

From there the story moves out of the realm of mythology and into history, as mystics throughout the ages have sought to rediscover the Tablets of Enoch - even by taking their own visionary trips into Heaven in the hopes of gaining a peek at the Celestial originals. Not only this, but the actual Books of Enoch (the Ethiopic Book and the later versions) were pushed underground by the Catholic Inquisitions. Thus, the same mystics yearned to find those lost books as well, in the hopes they contained clues into what Enoch himself had learned from the Angels.

John Dee was one of these mystics, and we find him asking the Angels about the lost books in his journals. (See Dee's *Fifth Book of the Mysteries*, April 18th, 1583) The Angels never promise to give Dee the *Ethiopic Book of Enoch*, but instead promise to deliver none other than the Celestial originals that Enoch had copied! The result was a lengthy text written in an indecipherable Angelic language called the *Book of the Speech of God*, or the *Book of Loagaeth*. This, claimed the Angels, was the re-introduction into human society of the lost wisdom of Enoch- and therefore the same book is also referred to as the *Book of Enoch* (aka the legendary *Tablets of Enoch*"). All of the magick Dee received from that point forward was based in some way upon the mysteries of Loagaeth itself. For this reason, and only this reason, Dee's journals and system of Magick is called *'Enochian'* - making his work a small subset of the larger Enochian genre that extends all the way back to Babylon.

So there, in a nutshell, is the historical and mythological context for Dee's Angelic work. As we can see, it is rooted entirely in Judeo-Christian literature and legend. There is nothing whatsoever to suggest that Dee was operating outside the world view of a devout Anglican Christian. However, what do his journals have to say about the entities to whom Dee and

Kelley were speaking? Do they stand outside of Christian myth and legend? Let us take a look:

Dee's Angelic journals begin on December 22, 1581 (see *The First Book of the Mysteries*) - somewhat before he met Edward Kelley while he still employed a medium by the name of Barnabus Saul. Saul sat before a crystal ball (called a *'shewstone'*) and gazed into its depths while Dee recited prayers in a nearby prayer room. After a while, an Angelic entity appeared in the stone and began to speak with the men. When asked to identify itself, the Angel gave its name as Annael. Was this the first name ever recorded in the famed *'Enochian'* Angelical tongue? Not at all - Annael (more commonly spelled Anael) is an Angel quite well known throughout Medieval/Renaissance magickal texts.

Anael is an Archangel, and a member of one of the most powerful Angelic Orders - the Seven Spirits who Stand Before God. (See *Revelations 4:5*: *"And out of the Throne proceeded lightnings and thunderings and voices: and there were seven lamps of fire burning before the throne, which are the seven Spirits of God."*) These seven Archangels are the chief governors of the entire universe, and they have appeared under different names and different forms throughout Biblical and Biblio-mystical literature. In nearly all cases, they are considered the Archangels of the seven ancient planets, the seven days of the week and the seven circles of Heaven.

One of the most popular mystical texts of Dee's time, which incorporates these seven powers, is called the *Heptameron: or Magical Elements*. The very name of the text indicates its focus upon the sacred number seven (*'hept-'* = *'seven'*) and the seven powers that govern the world. Both Dee and Kelley were quite familiar with this work, and drew from it in their own practices. Within its pages, we find the Seven Archangels listed as follows:

- Cassiel - Angel of Saturn
- Sachiel - Angel of Jupiter
- Camael - Angel of Mars
- Michael - Angel of the Sun
- Anael - Angel of Venus
- Raphael - Angel of Mercury
- Gabriel - Angel of the Moon

As we can see, Anael is the Angel of the planet Venus, and his name is likely a corruption of the Hebrew *'Haniel'* - meaning *'Joy of God'* or *'Grace of God'*. In both occultism and astrology, Venus is associated with joy and pleasure (especially of a sexual nature), as well as any passions bearing upon art, love, grace, beauty, etc. Therefore, Anael is the Archangel in charge of such aspects of Earthly life.

The next question we must ask is why this particular Angel chose to appear in the shewstone. Annael was not merely a random member of the seven highest Archangels, but is described by Dee as the *"Chief Governor General of this great period."* The meaning behind this obscure phrase is not found in the Heptameron, but within another popular mystical text of the time: the *Arbatel of Magic.*

The *Arbatel* is a very simple and eloquent grimoire from the late 1500s, outlining an occult philosophy based (in part) upon the sacred number seven. The Seven Spirits of God appear here as well, after a fashion - called in this case the seven *'Olympic Spirits'*. Just like the Archangels of the *Heptameron*, the Olympic Spirits are planetary in nature, so that each holds power over a specific astrological category of life.

Most importantly, these *'Spirits'* are described as successive governors of the world. All of them hold the same authority, but each of them assumes the role of chief of the group for an *'age'* of 490 years (or 7 times 70). According to the text, the Spirit of Saturn began his rule in 60 BCE, giving way to the Spirits of Jupiter, Mars and Sol in their turn. Beginning in 1411 CE, the Spirit of Venus (named Hagith) took control and would rule until 1900 CE. Therefore, Hagith was in charge when the Arbatel was written, and when Dee performed his séances.

The *'aphorisms'* or general rules of magick set forth in the Arbatel were absolutely foundational to Dee's understanding of magick. I would hazard to suggest the book is itself a primer for the magickal system that appears in his earliest magickal journals (the *Five Books of the Mysteries*). Dee called this magickal system the *Heptarchia* (or Seven-fold Rulership). It addresses the Angels of the seven planets, whom Dee referred to as the Kings and Princes of the world.

Thus, it is hardly surprising that Dee's very first Angelic contact was not only one of the Seven Archangels, but specifically the *'Chief Governor General of this great period'* as set forth in the *Arbatel* - the Angel of Venus. Dee had merely applied the philosophy of the Arbatel to the Seven Archangels of the *Heptameron* - preferring beings more familiar to a devout Christian. The Olympic Spirits were not only more obscure and lacking in Biblical justification, but the very term *'Olympic'* lent them a dangerously Pagan connotation.

At this point, we are still discussing the first entry of Dee's *Five Books* - December 22, 1583. Annael tells Dee and Saul how to proceed in further séances, and describes himself as the current governor set over the four Principal Archangels Michael, Gabriel, Raphael and Uriel. These latter four are considered second (or even equal) in power to the Seven Planetary Archangels, being set over the four classical Elements, the four Zodiacal Triplicities and the four quarters of the world. Three of the four (Michael, Gabriel and Raphael) are justified by direct mention in the canonical Bible, and legend holds that Michael and Gabriel actually sit at the right and left hands of God.

Annael promises that Dee will receive audience with these Angels, particularly Michael, and then promises not to appear again.

The journals do not pick up again until the following March (the 10th, 1582), when Sir Edward Talbot (aka Kelley) first appears as Dee's medium. As a test of Kelley's abilities, Dee set out to have him skry the Angel Anchor - one of a group of three Angels (Anchor, Anachor and Anilos) mentioned in some obscure occult literature of the time. Dee used the same methods of invocation he had employed with Saul, which soon resulted in the appearance of an Angel.

However, this Angel was not Anchor. When asked to identify itself, the being in the shewstone claimed to be none other than the Archangel Uriel, one of the four Principal Archangels in charge of the world. It is here that Dee begins to record the first bits of information that would become the *Five Books of the Mysteries* and the 'Heptarchic' system of magick.

There is perhaps some special significance to the fact that Uriel was the first of the big four to appear, in light of Dee's interest in Enochian legend. Though Dee could not have known it at the time, the lost *Ethiopic Book of Enoch* not only includes Uriel, but is perhaps the very origin of that Angel into Western occultism. In that text, Uriel is not actually one of the Principal Four - that honour is given to an Angel named Phanuel. (Because only three of the big four are mentioned in the Bible, various traditions have assigned the fourth position to different Angels.) However, Uriel is introduced to Enoch as nothing less than the director of the planets and all heavenly bodies in their natural courses. Therefore, it is quite appropriate for Uriel to appear first for Dee and Kelley, and to both launch and supervise the transmission of the Heptarchic planetary-based system of magick.

Over the hundreds of pages that follow in Dee's journals, it is Uriel that appears to be in charge of the séances. When the men failed in some way, upsetting the Angels, it was most often Uriel who appeared in the stone to chastise them. More importantly, it is Uriel who introduces the men to the other Principal Archangels - each of whom were in charge of transmitting some specific aspect of the magickal system.

First was Michael (as promised by Annael), whose primary job seems to have been to reveal the magickal furniture and equipment that would be needed for the remainder of the work. Later came Raphael, who transmitted the entire text of the *Book of Loagaeth* (Dee's own *Book of Enoch*) - and therefore was first to reveal some form of the famous Angelical Language. After him came Gabriel, who was in charge of the transmission of the 48 Angelical Keys that promised to unlock the mysteries of *Loagaeth*.

After *Loagaeth* was complete, we find the material that is most often considered *'Enochian'*- the records beyond the *Five Books of the Mysteries* and its *Heptarchia*. This is where we find such things as the *'91 Parts of the Earth'* and the *'Four Watchtowers'* (more accurately called the *'Great Table of the Earth'*.) These aspects of Dee's magick were delivered by Angels unknown to Biblical literature and legend, but these Angels were appointed to their tasks specifically by the four Archangels themselves.

Let me take a brief moment to summarize what we have seen thus far. First, John Dee desired to speak directly with Biblical Angels. As he states very clearly in the preface to his *Five Books of the Mystery*:

> *"I have read in thy books, and records, how Enoch enjoyed thy favour and conversation. With Moses thou wast familiar. And also that to Abraham, Isaac and Jacob, Joshua, Gideon, Esdras, Daniel, Tobias and sundry others, thy good Angels were sent, by thy disposition to instruct them, inform them, help them, yea in worldly and domestic affairs, yea and sometimes to satisfy their desires, doubts and questions of thy Secrets."*

Not only this, but Dee had a particular interest in the legends of Enoch and hopes of recovering the lost Enochian wisdom. To this end, he made first contact with the Archangel he assumed to be in charge of the entire world - Annael, the Angel of Venus. That Archangel, then, gave him contact with the four Archangels Michael, Gabriel, Raphael and Uriel. It was these four who directed the transmission of the entire corpus of 'Enochian' magick contained in Dee's records.

Why is it, then, that modern occultists have become convinced that Dee was not speaking with traditional Angels at all? Perhaps we feel intellectually superior when we suggest that Dee was deluding himself - seeing Biblical Angels merely because he expected to see them, and never properly questioned their true identities. However, I find two places to play devil's advocate to that view:

First, I note that no-one has made these same accusations about the authors of texts like the *Heptameron*, Agrippa's *Three Books of Occult Philosophy*, the *Fourth Book of Occult Philosophy* and countless other mystical texts that mention the very same Angels. If we are going to accuse Dee of delusion about who he was speaking with, then should we not direct the same doubts toward every mystical text? And if not, why not? My assumption is that *'Dee-doubting'* is merely a fad among occult scholars and students, without any solid foundation.

Second, I note that - unlike the texts mentioned above - Dee's records are very extensive. He does not merely present us with a name, description and sigil for each Angel he contacts, but actually scribes page after page of long-winded sermons, visions, speeches and conversations with each spiritual entity listed. Do these records show forth very un-Christian beings who lie to Dee at every turn? Quite the contrary. While some of what the Angels had to say may have been considered heretical to the politically-driven authorities of the Catholic and Anglican Churches, I find the records are abundant with the kind of material one would expect to hear in any church on Sunday morning. I also find the Angels' messages to be very straightforward and unwavering, while it is Dee and Kelley themselves who often misinterpret the Angels based on their own egos and earthly desires.

Of course, at the very beginning of this essay I admitted that Dee did, in fact, contact many unique entities. However, based on everything you have read thus far, I called it misleading to insist that Dee was not in contact with traditional Biblical Angels. An old Qabalistic axiom states that *"every blade of grass has over it an Angel bidding it 'Grow.'"* Even the classical magickal texts speak of entire legions of Angels and spirits who are subservient to the more well-known Angelic beings. Dee's work is no exception to this rule, and several of the Archangels introduced the men to their own subservients- such as those who delivered the later bits of the Enochian system.

More often than not, modern texts about Enochian magick tend to focus upon these subservient Angels, even to the exclusion of the Archangels themselves. Perhaps the non-traditional Angels are simply more interesting. Perhaps modern occult authors simply wish to avoid making Enochian magick seem *'too Christian.'* Whatever the cause, I feel this practice removes Dee's work from its proper place within Renaissance Angel Magick, and it certainly helps perpetuate the growing fallacy that Dee and Kelley were speaking to something non-Angelic, something alien, something called *'the Enochians.'*

At this point I must, reluctantly, bring this short essay to a close. It is my hope that, to some extent, I have shed light onto a rather obscure facet of Dee's extensive body of magickal literature. I hope that I have helped solidify the true definition of the term *'Enochian'* - not as the designation of Dee's system of magick, but as a classification of a larger genre of literature, the same way we use terms such as *'Solomonic'* or *'Gothic'* or even *'Shakespearean.'*

I have merely given a general overview of the truly Angelic nature of Dee's work and the entities with whom he was in contact. It is vital to view his magickal journals against the backdrop of traditional Western mysticism - with all of its Christian elements- as this is the same tradition from which texts like the *Heptameron* and the *Arbatel of Magic* arise. And such Western mystical texts, in turn, form the foundation of Dee's own body of work.

EDWARD KELLEY PERFORMING NECROMANCY IN A CHURCHYARD

Madeline Montalban, Elemental and Fallen Angels

"I mean, aren't angels supposed to be rather gentle and helpful and all that?"

By Julia Phillips

"You're doing what Marcellus warned you against," Richardson said, "judging them by English pictures. All nightgowns and body and a kind of flacculent sweetness. As in cemeteries, with broken bits of marble. These are Angels – not a bit the same thing. These are the principles of the tiger and the volcano, and the flaming suns of space."

(Charles Williams, *The Place of the Lion*)

When I first encountered angelic beings my reaction was along the lines of, *"whoa! What was that?!"* The energy came through exactly like a volcano, or a flaming sun of space. It wasn't frightening (although in hindsight perhaps it should have been), but it was completely overwhelming. Fortunately I had built up to this first encounter over a period of years through a system of Hermetic training, so I was able to negotiate the rather bumpy ride without gaining too many metaphysical bruises.

I say *'first encounter'*, but perhaps that should be *'first deliberate encounter'*, because I had been aware of angelic entities for as long as I can remember. I never thought of them specifically as angels, though; perhaps because my experiences were so different to those classic images of cute angels; *'all nightgowns and body and a kind of flacculent sweetness.'*

The correlation clicked in my mind once I started deliberately to make contact with angelic entities. I recognised the energy pattern immediately and realised that through my ritual practice, I was formalising something I had been doing instinctively most of my life. Not just formalising of course, as I was also taking control of my journey rather than just following where my whim led me. I like to wander and meander along interesting byways as much as the next person, but sometimes following a map has some advantages.

Possibly because the formal approach came after the personal one I tend to be rather idiosyncratic when it comes to the practical aspect of my ritual work. I have studied the classic texts and ritual forms, but the complexity of (for example) the Enochian system is not my preferred way to enter into a relationship with the angels. I have practised Enochian ritual and have a profound respect for it, but my personal approach is a little less formal, a little more instinctive.

I have recently written a biography of Madeline Montalban,[14] who is best known to the general public as the contributor on tarot and astrology for *Prediction* magazine between 1953 and her death in 1982. To occultists though, she is better known for the training system she developed to help seekers to contact and work with the angels.

During the research for the biography I spoke with her students and close friends, and all of them mentioned Madeline's strong connection with the angelic forces. Her correspondence course was created around very sound principles to provide people with the basic tools to make their own connection. Madeline didn't expect her students to copy her word for word, but to use the techniques to make their own way.

---

14 To be published by Neptune Press

This is a very classic Hermetic technique, where an understanding of spiritual mysteries is achieved through encouragement by a *'teacher'* and a group of fellow-travellers. I place *'teacher'* in inverted commas because in the Hermetic tradition, the role is one of facilitator rather than guru – the teacher does not pretend to have any special insight or knowledge, just experience of a technique that anyone can use to achieve a personal gnosis of some kind.

Madeline's techniques were based on years of study of primary source material, but she created her own unique approach to the practice of working with angelic beings. Perhaps one of the reasons that I have always felt so close to Madeline is that this is essentially my own approach. I have studied the texts and considered the techniques that other people find useful, but in practice I find it more effective to use my own methods.

Before considering the pros and cons of different methods though, my first question is, *'why angels?'* Why would anyone, me included, want to attempt to contact these entities – always assuming of course that they even exist and are not a figment of the imagination?

I put this point because it is always possible that what I and others experience has a rational, scientific explanation and *'angel'* is simply a way of describing something for which we currently have no other words. Much like electricity before its principles were understood; its effects could be seen, measured, and even used in some way, but it was a primitive explanation lacking real understanding of the true nature of the force of electricity.

Angels could be something similar; our interpretation of them could be just a naïve attempt to explain the inexplicable. On the other hand, they could be entities whose relationship with humans spans thousands of years. I'm open to all possibilities and in the absence of any final proof I choose to follow my intuition. This means that I will write about angels and human interaction with them as a reality, but the reader should make up his or her own mind on the matter.

I am certain that some of the contributors to this book will look in detail at the literary evidence and myths relating to angels, so will restrict myself here to consideration of those angels that are generally lumped into the *'fallen'* category as it is here that my own particular interest is focused.

Naturally, the only place to start is with that most famous of rebel angels, God's chief antagonist, Lucifer. Or is he?

The journey of Helel ben Shahar to Prince of Darkness is a curious and fascinating one. We know that the conflation of the Canaanite deity associated with Venus, the Morning Star, with the Christian concept of a Devil, began with a translation choice:

> *"How art thou fallen from heaven, O day-star, son of the morning! How art thou cut down to the ground, that didst cast lots over the nations!"*

In this famous verse (12) from chapter 14 of the *Book of Isaiah, Helel ben Shahar* (*'Helel, son of the morning'*) was translated as Lucifer (or Lucifera to use the more common feminine form of the word) in the very influential fourth century Latin Vulgate. This word was much in evidence in classical literature as a reference to Venus, the Morning Star, and its use by the translator of the Vulgate, St Jerome, in *Isaiah* was apt and logical. The ensuing journey from Light-bringer to Prince of Darkness was not quite so logical, however, but fascinating as it is, a detailed exploration falls well outside the scope of this current chapter. Suffice it to say that whilst the New Testament refers to angels, demons, Beelzebub and Satan, there is no mention of any explicit relationship between any of these and the one known as Lucifer or the Light-bringer.

Whilst Lucifer's identification as a *'fallen angel'* is misleading however, there are others who are quite clearly and accurately identified within angelic lore in the *Book of Enoch*[15] as this extract from chapter VI shows:

> *"2. And the angels, the children of the heaven, saw and lusted after them, and said to one another: 'Come, let us choose us wives from among the children of men and beget us children.'*
>
> *3. And Semjâzâ, who was their leader, said unto them: 'I fear ye will not indeed agree to do this deed, and I alone shall have to pay the penalty of a great sin.'*
>
> *4. And they all answered him and said: 'Let us all swear an oath, and all bind ourselves by mutual imprecations not to abandon this plan but to do this thing.'*
>
> *5. Then swore they all together and bound themselves by mutual imprecations upon it.*
>
> *6. And they were in all two hundred; who descended in the days of Jared on the summit of Mount Hermon, and they called it Mount Hermon, because they had sworn and bound themselves by mutual imprecations upon it.*
>
> *7. And these are the names of their leaders: Sêmîazâz, their leader, Arâkîba, Râmêêl, Kôkabîêl, Tâmîêl, Râmîêl, Dânêl, Êzêqêêl, Barâqîjâl, Asâêl, Armârôs, Batârêl, Anânêl, Zaqîêl, Samsâpêêl, Satarêl, Tûrêl, Jômjâêl, Sariêl."*

Alternative spellings abound for the names but the essence of the story is that an angel called Samyaza or Shemyaza led a number of other angels to visit earth in physical form. Once there they took wives (implying a male gender for the angels), produced children, and taught humans many skills:[16]

> *"1. And Azâzêl taught men to make swords, and knives, and shields, and breastplates, and made known to them the metals of the earth and the art of working them, and bracelets, and ornaments, and the use of*

---

15 The Book of Enoch is a pseudoepigraphal work (a work that claims to be by a biblical character). The Book of Enoch was not included in either the Hebrew or most Christian biblical canons, but could have been considered a sacred text by the sectarians. The original Aramaic version was lost until the Dead Sea fragments were discovered. (Milik, Jazef. T., ed.)
16 Book of Enoch, Chapter VIII

antimony, and the beautifying of the eyelids, and all kinds of costly stones, and all colouring tinctures.

2. And there arose much godlessness, and they committed fornication, and they were led astray, and became corrupt in all their ways. Semjâzâ taught enchantments, and root-cuttings, Armârôs the resolving of enchantments, Barâqîjâl, taught astrology, Kôkabêl the constellations, Êzêqêêl the knowledge of the clouds, Araqiêl the signs of the earth, Shamsiêl the signs of the sun, and Sariêl the course of the moon."

In other words, the angels taught humans practical skills and revealed mysteries, and in procreating with humans they created hybrid offspring; for what purpose we can only conjecture. The *Book of Enoch* tells us that the offspring of these pairings between human and angel resulted in a race of giants known as the Nephilim. The biological results of hybridisation can be varied, but it is not uncommon for positive heterosis to produce hybrids that are stronger or bigger.

The four archangels, Michael, Uriel, Raphael and Gabriel, saw all this activity and went to God saying:[17]

*"6. Thou seest what Azâzêl hath done, who hath taught all unrighteousness on earth **and revealed the eternal secrets which were (preserved) in heaven, which men were striving to learn:**" (my emphasis)*

The God of Enoch did not approve of angels revealing heaven's *'eternal secrets'* to humans. It was the Garden of Eden all over again but this time God sent the four archangels to warn Noah of the flood that he intended to visit upon the earth to destroy all humans and Nephilim alike, and told them to bind Azazel, Shemyaza and the other angels and cast them into:

"...the abyss of fire: and to the torment and the prison in which they shall be confined forever."

---

17 Ibid, Chapter IX

We can only speculate why these secrets and the other skills taught by the angels were considered to be so dangerous, but clearly heaven's *'eternal secrets'* had to be protected at all costs, at least as far as God and the Archangels were concerned.

This is not the place for a detailed examination of the Book of Enoch, but it was necessary to give this background in order to answer the question I posed above: why would anyone, me included, want to contact an angel?

The answer for me is that I have an unquenchable curiosity and I love to learn new skills. The angels in Enoch wanted to share their knowledge with humans, so it is logical for me to seek them out in the hope that they might continue the process that was interrupted when the Archangels bound them and cast them into what sounds awfully like the Christian version of hell.

There are a number of different techniques available to people who want to seek out the angels, ranging from very simple to very complex methods. In my experience, they all work provided the technique is used properly and with clear intent. The choice of technique depends more upon personal preferences – if you like, some of us prefer to use email, others use a telephone, and some people still prefer to handwrite letters. The contact is made no matter what the method, but the response can vary depending on a range of circumstances. Following my analogy, it takes longer to handwrite a letter, post it, and wait for a reply, than calling someone by telephone or sending/receiving an email. It all works, it just works differently.

There is also consideration of which of the angels to contact. As I said above, I have a particular interest in the angels that are considered to be *'fallen'*, but I also have a very strong connection with the elemental angels – of which, more below. Other people may focus more upon angels associated with planetary energies, or those found within the classical cosmologies – for example, the Seraphim or the Archangels.

This is not usually so much a rational choice as one that is driven by a particular experience that an individual has with one or more angelic beings. The decision is not so much which angel to choose, as whether to accept the contact that has occurred and follow where that might lead. This might be through visionary experiences or dreams, but it is just as likely to result from a study of the angels using one of the traditional sources found in theology or magic (or both).

The correspondence courses that Madeline Montalban taught were intended to lead humans from the darkness of ignorance to the light of knowledge. The correspondence courses introduced students to a number of different angels, each associated with a planet and various attributions of colours, plants, animals, scents, and so on, which helps the student to attune to the energy of an angel and work harmoniously to achieve desired outcomes.

Madeline herself built a strong relationship with an angel that she knew as Lumiel, a variation on the better known Lucifer. Lumiel made his first appearance in course number 12 (of 42), and the mythology that Madeline describes in that course is a very personal one that she developed over many years.

What is most important though is that in studying the courses, students are inspired to make their own contact with the angels, not just reproduce what Madeline herself achieved. It is this more than anything that sets Madeline Montalban apart from so many of her contemporaries; she didn't want brainless followers; she wanted her students to be thinking, rational human beings who were every bit as committed as she was to exploring the mystery and seeking knowledge. She gave tools, not answers.

Although I studied the angelic course material and worked my way through the various exercises, my own core technique for contacting angels is rooted in a system of guided visualisation called Hermetics. It is an oral tradition and the few of us who have studied it do not really know where it came from. Parts of it are easily identifiable from classic texts and traditions of magic, but the overall structure and methodology is unique and unclassifiable.

The very early exercises in Hermetics lead the traveller to visit the Elemental realms of Fire, Water, Air and Earth. Specific gateways are used and once in the Elemental realm, the traveller meets various inhabitants including the Elemental King, Angel, and Ruler.

The Elemental Angels are typical of their kind in many ways, but in my experience have a quite different role to, for example, the Archangels. Because there is so little written about the Elemental Angels, my knowledge of them comes primarily from personal interaction. That is perfectly adequate for my own purposes, but the reader must decide whether or not it is adequate in a wider sense.

I have been working with the Elemental angels since the mid 1980s, so I have a long personal history with them. What my workings have led me to consider is that perhaps all angels have the same heritage and power, but that they are differentiated on a functional basis. In this hypothesis the Archangel Uriel is no more intrinsically powerful than (for example) Aral, the Angel of the Fire Element, but each has a different role and function within the universe.

This theory is not completely consistent with some of the theological thinking on angelic hierarchies – for example, the *Celestial Hierarchy* of Pseudo-Dionysius or the *Summa Theologica* by Aquinas – which posit that angels are ranked according to their respective powers, although even here there is a functional differentiation. It is, however, my practical experience and in the absence of any evidence to the contrary, it is my accepted theory for the moment. Of course everything is subject to change in the light of new facts or experiences.

My interaction with the elemental angels has led to a number of instances of what I refer to as *'Eureka'* moments; a blinding insight into something that had previously been obscured by either lack of knowledge of its existence, or misperceptions about its actuality. Perhaps the most awe inspiring of these moments was a revelation by the Angel of the Water Element about the nature of water and its function within the universe. This is not the place to delve into that realisation in any detail, but it is the place to suggest that anyone could achieve a *'Eureka'* moment by engaging with these angels. In my experience they are very agreeable to revealing *'heaven's eternal secrets'* to those who are willing to listen.

And this brings us neatly full circle to the angels who were (according to Enoch) damned by God for daring to reveal these eternal secrets to humanity.

Accepting that the basis for this is an apocryphal text that may well be nothing more than mythical poetry, it is extraordinary what a strong grip that the concept of fallen angels has on human consciousness. They inspire strong feelings from revulsion to worship, and are often held to be responsible for tempting mankind away from following a righteous path laid down by God. Or perhaps we should say, laid down by those who wrote the *'word of God'*. As far as I know, God himself is rather silent on the matter.

I have known a lot of people over the years who share my interest in the angels, and especially the so-called fallen angels. Over the past ten years or so however, I have noticed a marked increase in their number, and more to the point, an increase in the number of people who wish to practise ritual magic in order to contact these beings. Sometimes this is intellectual curiosity sparked by some research trail, but a sizeable number seem to have been inspired by visionary experiences.

This is a significant point for me, as I have always thought that personal experience of an entity is more important than what other people may have to say about it. Not to discount the work of philosophers and magicians of the past, but in my view a personal vision or experience has equal (if not greater) validity and should always be given due credibility and authority.

The increasing incidence of angelic visions, especially those focused around Shemyaza and Azazel (and others similar to these two angels), leads me to believe that the time is right for humanity to seek out the *'eternal mysteries'* that the angels shared with our forebears thousands of years ago. In the past it was the angels who came to us; perhaps this time they are waiting for us to go to them.

Bibliography
Milik, Jazef. T. (ed); *The Books of Enoch: Aramaic Fragments of Qumran Cave 4*; 1976; Oxford
Williams, Charles; *The Place of the Lion*; 1947; Victor Gollancz Ltd; London

WITH KIND PERMISSION OF THE ARTIST, DIANA ALLAM, (C) 2009

AZAZEL & SHEMYAZA

Sex, Drugs & Rock 'n' Roll

By Diana Allam

This essays is about my relationship with two Fallen Angels known as Azazel & Shemyaza, aka the Peacock Angel, or Leader of the Watcher Angels. This personal relationship was built over many years of deep level hermetic meditational work, which has formed my personal Angelic Mythology.

What is a Fallen Angel? To me a Fallen Angel is one that has been separated from the Divine. If you have a channel of communication open with the Divine, and that communication suddenly ends, then the resulting separation is an immensely painful and upsetting experience. This happened to me, and was my Fall from Grace. Fallen Angels are the ones that chose this separation; they did this so that they could teach humanity, and impart knowledge to help mankind evolve. However, this was supposedly against the will of God, and holds a key to free will, free will being the key to understanding the fall of the angels, and fundamentally linked with the mythology of the Garden of Eden, and the fall of man.

Imagine the sacrifice they made for us, when I contemplate this I certainly do not see fallen angels as bad or evil. To me the whole idea of fallen angels being devils or demons is negative propaganda. For humanity to evolve on the journey back to the Divine, one must have an understanding of all parts of *The Self*; light and dark, yin and yang, good and bad. To *'Know thyself'* is vitally important for anyone on a magical path.

Often, when people get into angels it's the good, fluffy, pink and wholly positive ones that they refer to; any mention of fallen angels, (particularly Lucifer) and they recoil with fear. Many do not want to see their dark or shadow sides, for these negative aspects of the self are very challenging. Lucifer is a Light Bringer, he illuminates the dark, all that was hidden is revealed. If this is understood then these angels will be seen as beacons of light within the darkness.

Some people associate Azazel & Shemyaza with Lucifer, or think that they are one and the same, but I see them more like brothers, and Lucifer as a different entity entirely. Azazel is Shemyaza's shadow side, I first met Azazel on a beach in an hermetic meditation; he was dressed in dark purple leather with wispy shards of purple and black smoke spiralling around him. I felt no fear or evil, just sexual energy. He was like every female's fantasy in one package – Johnny Depp as Captain Jack, a Russian Cossack, or an Arabian Prince, and to this day he is my Sex, Drugs and Rock 'n' Roll. When Azazel left me in the meditation Shemyaza appeared. Shemyaza is huge, and fills the whole sky, his colours are sky blue and white, his energy is fatherly and loving, he is my husband and Azazel is my lover, this is the only way I can describe their energies.

Whenever I work magically I bring in Azazel, and automatically Michael will appear. Michael doesn't slay dragons, for me he is the great balancer. And when these two join together, Bang!, a whole new being 'becomes'. For me it is all about balancing the dark with the light, but before we can balance anything we must illuminate the darkness, so that we may truly fulfil the maxim 'know thyself', by knowing all of ourselves.

THIRTEEN UNICYCLES
IN THE WOODS
By Adele Nozedar

'Then delivered my soul shall learn
A darker knowledge and in hatred turn
From every thought of God mankind has had.
Thought is a garment and the soul's a bride
That cannot in that trash and tinsel hide:
Hatred of God may bring the soul to God'

(W.B. Yeats)

Elusive creatures, these angels. Not only hard to pin down (probably because there are thousands of them capering about on the head of the pin you're trying to stick them with), but a mass of contradictions. Large, small; benevolent, fearsome; peaceful, vengeful. Maybe, to understand what exactly these creatures are, we need to accept the limitations of our human realms of perception, to grope, fumbling in the dark, for the place both inside and outside of ourselves that can operate under a different remit. We need to make a leap, to extend our senses further than the sweet little picket fenced garden that we call *'sanity'*.

When Eve gave Adam the *'fruit of wisdom'*, she encouraged him to extend his senses, too, to understand that there was a bigger world out there than the one that their terribly jealous God had wanted them to confine them in. Choice, awareness of that choice, and freedom to make those choices. Freedom to come back into the garden of Heaven and freedom to roam the cold empty corridors of Hell.

Exploration from the safety of the garden can take whatever form you like. For thousands of years, we've sought different ways to unlock the gates, the doors of perception. We can smash them apart for a minute with the application of psychedelics and hallucinogens; we can try to ease them gently open by the diligent application of, say, yoga and abstinence. For some, the reconciliation of the self after such experiences can be difficult to master.

Sometimes, for a time, the doors open in other ways; death, grief, a moment of extreme need. Occasionally, they open unbidden and unexpectedly for no apparent reason at all.

Once, I saw one of the things that we call an angel. And I also saw one of the things we call a demon. These visitations were one of the latter experiences; unexpected, unbidden, no grief, no drugs, no drink, no ascetic practises.

To give you some context in view of what I've said already, and in surprising contrast to many of my generation, I've never taken any psychedelics. I did once eat some cannabis resin in Amsterdam in the early '80s and watched the colours peel off the walls and people turn into animals. More recently, I ate some magic mushrooms with a good friend and we clinically recorded exactly what was happening. Sad, eh? I do practise yoga from time to time, and have fasted, but certainly not in any extreme way.

Here's my account of what I saw.

Four years ago, in that desultory no-man's land between Christmas and New Year, I was walking the dogs at the edge of a forest plantation. It was a low cloud cover, dismal, muddy sort of Welsh day, the kind that you know you'll feel nostalgic about once you're old and too infirm for such ramblings.

As I walked along, I was looking left into the plantation, not for any particular reason. To the right was open heath land and the mountain beyond, obscured by cloud. I stopped at the beginning of one of the long, hummocky grooves between the regimented rows of trees. Maybe about 50-100 yards away there was a gap in the pattern of the branches, where a patch of half-hearted light was coming through. Something seemed to be moving in the gap. As I watched, with my dogs equally attentive and focussed, a form started to appear. It emerged, absorbing the light into itself to give it shape, an Angel. Distinctly male, muscular, powerful, suspended in the trees. A proper, classic, Old Testament style Angel, no messing about or ambiguity. It was burning with light, absolutely burning with a sort of fire that became stronger and stronger until I had to look at it obliquely and certainly not all at once.

At the time, we just watched until the vision faded away, and then I found myself sitting down in the mud and weeping, shaking with cold and fear.

I recovered, and set off back for home. Luckily, everyone was out and I had a hot bath and went back to sleep to recover from the shock and to try to work it out in my dreams.

I didn't tell anyone about this, and I'll tell you why. Just a couple of days earlier I'd once again been walking the dogs, and I saw 13 unicyclists coming towards me along a bit of old railway track. We had to step aside for them as they came past, I bantered jovially with them. Of course I was very excited about such a weird encounter and told everyone about it as soon as I got home. But the guests who were staying here thought I was making it up! After all, 13 unicycles in the middle of an obscure track in mid Wales is a bit of a stretch. So, coming back a couple of days later and telling everyone there was a classically-styled and rather terrifying Angel suspended in the woods just wasn't going to cut muster. There was another reason, too. This felt like a very private experience, and sometimes, talking about something can sort of make it disseminate its potency.

Here's where the story gets REALLY weird, and as I write I'm still wondering whether I'll press the 'send' button on my laptop or scrap the entire contribution to this book.

The next day, I took the same route. No change in the weather; misty, mizzly, muddy. I stopped to look at the place where I'd seen the angel. Nothing. I was sort of disappointed, but aware at the same time that I'd been given a glimpse of something very rare and shouldn't really be looking for further *'evidence'*, (although evidence of what, I can't really say). The patch of sky that had shone through the space in the branches was dark. I looked towards it, remembering. As I did so, the darkness gained in intensity, almost palpable, like when a cloud goes across the sun. Except that there WAS no sun. This time, the shape that formed this time in the gap in the branches was that of a demon or devil; again, classic in form, although bigger than you might think, with a tail and a pitchfork and short stubby horns. The devil shape was easier to see than that of the angel; there was no blinding fire, just deep, swampy darkness. In the same way that the light had mustered itself together to create the angel, the darkness did the same thing with the devil; except the darkness was less violent, easier to look at. And perhaps the oddest thing of all was that the devil was far less terrifying than the angel. I could look at it him easily; oh, and again, he was distinctly male.

There was more of an acceptance, this time. The shock of seeing the angel was profound, and so I was a bit more prepared for this new revelation.

How did this affect me? Well, until now, when I'm giving up this secret, it gave me one more very private experience to ponder on. I didn't go running off looking for any more angels, or demons; I was already fascinated but now I have something more than an intellectual idea, which further fuels that fascination.

My impressions?

There wasn't any conflict between the two figures that occupied the same space, whatever that space WAS, whether physical or metaphysical, *'real'* in the sense that our immediate impressions are 'real', or belonging to that other world, the one outside the picket fence.

I guess we've all read about an eternal 'war' between Angels and Demons for Men's souls, a battle between these mighty, supernatural opposing forces which has lasted since time began. I don't know if this is actually true, but I suspect it is a metaphor for something else. I'm not sure that I subscribe to the theory that the Earth is like one long time-share between the forces of Good and Evil, where the booking dates have got all mixed up and the Angels and Demons are locked in an eternal squabble over the sun loungers on the beach (i.e., our souls). This doesn't sit right with me. Whilst most of us have an innate sense of knowing what is right or wrong, since what's right are those things that work for society as a whole, I certainly don't believe that the true demarcation between what's good and what's evil are necessarily so clearly delineated. Applying dark to one and light to another are all part of the illusion. The 'trash and tinsel' that W.B. Yeats mentions.

I suspect that our angels and our demons – or 'fallen' angels, angels gone wrong – have to be embraced as equally important parts of the picture, essential to our balance and understanding, and whether they are within us or outside of us is really of no account. Perhaps the 'dark angel' was easier to look at since he is made from matter, like us, a part of the material world in which we live for the time being. The 'light angel' was impossible to see properly because the he's more distinctly from the other world.

I don't know.

I'm still thinking. And I feel very lucky to have seen these creatures. I just wish that someone else had seen them with me.

XVII

The Star

THE STAR, SIDHE TAROT, BY EMILY CARDING

THE SALVATION OF THE SIDHE
Emily Carding

*"We could cut off half the human race, but would not,
for we are expecting salvation"*

(*Fairy Faith in Celtic Countries*, Evans-Wentz)

The Faery race has been a source of fascination, joy and
inspiration throughout history, but also the source of at least as
much fear and distrust. Normally portrayed in modern times as
diminutive, girlish figures clad in flower petals, (and often stripy
socks for some reason), with beautiful luminescent wings, belief
in their kind today is often ridiculed. But anyone who has any
sense of a realm beyond the physical knows that such magical
beings are not only very real, they are also far more powerful
than their commercialized popular image implies. Now, I know
plenty of people who have indeed seen this kind of tiny, winged
fairy and I have no doubt that there are certain nature spirits
which appear in this way to those who are fortunate enough to
see them. However the most ancient tales tell of a tall and noble
race, possessing their own culture, rules and structured society.
They are known throughout the Celtic lands by many names;
the Gentry, the Shining Ones, the Cousins and the Tylwyth Teg.
The name which I most often use is the *Sidhe*. There is much
written of the Sidhe throughout Celtic mythology and folklore
and yet their true origins remain shrouded in mystery. It is
widely believed by those who accept their existence that they
pre-date humanity by some considerable time and there are
many theories as to where their tale begins. Are they a memory

of an ancient race, the Tuatha de Danaan, who used their magic to retreat into the hills when defeated by the Milesians? Or does their story in fact go even further back? Could it be that their true and distant origins were in fact not earthly at all, but heavenly?

Heavenly! That's a loaded term for a pagan. And yet as a pagan there is no question that there are such things as Angels: these intensely powerful cosmic forces are rather difficult not to notice when you're working the kind of magick that requires their cooperation or attracts their attention! It is easy enough to see the Judeo-Christian framework as one layer of a deeper cosmic truth which includes both Angels and Faeries.

It is almost certain that both races of beings are an integral part of nature and the Universe, and so pre-date humanity and our various belief systems by a significant amount of time, but the human mind needs structures and frameworks in order to try and understand the enormity of the multiverse and our place in it. I hold a shamanic point of view, thinking in terms of Upper World, Middle World and Under World and the various realms that exist within them. Therefore Angels are agents of the Upper World, and the Sidhe have their realm in the Under World even though they have often been encountered in intangible form in the Middle World. It has always been my perception that the Angels and the Sidhe have much in common, (apart from both having their image horribly de-empowered by ridiculous New Age gurus, that is). As the name Shining Ones implies, the Sidhe have a powerful inner light. Like Angels, they often appear tall, fair and beautiful and also like angels they have the power to assume other forms. An obvious similarity is that they are both perceived to be winged beings, (though most Faery beings I have encountered have been wingless.) In fact it seems likely that the marvellously aesthetically pleasing shape that is presented to us bears little resemblance to their true form. There is a commonality of symbolism between them; the heptagram being associated with both Faeries and Angels. Another connection, though tenuous, is the red and white roses. In the Faery tradition, these represent the rivers of blood and tears, the primal forces of creation and destruction which flow through the Under World. I have also seen them used to represent the male and female polarity of Lucifer and Lilith.

Both Angels and the Sidhe are known for their inhumanly beautiful singing and for their ability to aid humans if it suits their purpose or mood, or hinder if it does not. There is a certain noble aloofness and extraordinary power in both. The Sidhe are associated with starlight, indeed they have a great love of the stars of the upper world, which may once have been their home. Ritual magicians use similar techniques to call on Faeries and Angels, so it is not a great stretch of the imagination to conceive of the Faery race as being Fallen Angels.

But this is not merely a theory based on imaginings and supposition. The folklore of the Celtic lands is absolutely littered with references to the fall of the Faery race from Heaven. W.Y. Evans-Wentz's *The Fairy Faith in Celtic Countries* contains numerous accounts of people from all over the Celtic landscape who fervently believed that Faeries are Angels that were cast out of Heaven when Lucifer and his followers rebelled against God. From the Scottish Highlands comes this verse, reputedly sung by the Sidhe:

> *"Not of the seed of Adam are we,*
> *Nor is Abraham our Father,*
> *But of the seed of the Proud Angel,*
> *Driven forth from Heaven"*

The tale varies a little in every telling, but essentially remains the same. Lucifer, gathering a host of supporters, rebels against God and leaves to establish his own kingdom. Either the force of all those Angels leaving heaven so abruptly, or through loyalty and support for Lucifer, Heaven begins to empty. In order to prevent Heaven being emptied completely, God orders the gates to be shut, commanding that, *"Those who are out remain* out, *those who are in remain in.*" Those Angels who had left Heaven but did not wish to join Lucifer are doomed to inhabit the hollow places of the Earth until Judgement day when they expect salvation. These Angels become the Sidhe.

This is an ancient myth passed down to children sat on their grandparent's knees for many generations and it is truly fascinating. Although it would not do to over analyse any myth, it is interesting to look behind the Christian imagery and think about what this might mean on a level of spiritual truth. Is this just a creation of the Church wishing to demonise the old pagan practices by associating them yet again with the Devil, or is there more to it? You could say the same about stories of changelings and the malicious behaviour of Faery beings often cited in folklore and yet anyone who has had any real depth of contact with Faery knows well that they can display great cruelty and heartlessness with one hand while they bestow inspiration and joy with the other. I have even heard from reliable sources of one or two changelings in modern times, so it is my feeling that there is also much more to this tale than priestly propaganda.

R.J. Stewart gives real insight into the deeper levels of this myth through a brief comment in his book, *The Well of Light*. When mentioning this myth he calls it a *'dogmatic rationalization'* of an ancient creation myth and goes on to say that *"Light from the spiritual dimensions 'falls' into the body of the planet and many lesser but powerful spiritual beings fall with the Light."* This is a theme that we can see throughout mythology and mystery traditions, most notably in the fall of Sophia. If we think of *'God'* as the source of spiritual light and Lucifer in the true meaning of his name as the *'Light-bringer,'* then we may be looking at the spiritual birth of the planet with the Sidhe as sparks of the living spirit of the planet itself. When working with Faery allies on a couple of occasions I have seen the most brilliant falling star, which certainly felt like a signature of the Sidhe. The *'salvation'* that they supposedly await on judgement day hints to the spiritual awakening of the light within the world. Returning to *The Fairy Faith*, there are a few accounts which mention the possible return of the Sidhe to the surface of the Earth. For example:

> *"...they have been commanded to inhabit the places named for a certain period of time, and when it is expired before the consummation of the world, they will be seen as numerous as ever."*

One of the most intriguing contemporary accounts of Faery contact can be seen in John Matthews' *The Sidhe*, a most convincing piece of channelled writing in which the author engages in conversation with a representative of the Faery race. This being also mentions an impending time of re-emergence for the Sidhe:

> *"We believe that a new era may be about to dawn in which the people of the Sidhe will come forth again and be seen by all."*

It is a well-known element of Judgement day that Angels make themselves visible to mankind, so here we have another connection. If we look at the Tarot card *Judgement*, which in traditional decks directly relates to the biblical event, it has many levels of meaning. Presuming that we are not going to interpret it as meaning that the surface of the world is about to be overrun by zombies, the Judgement card can indicate a step forward in the spiritual evolution of an individual, an increased level of awareness and a deeper knowledge of the true nature of self. On a global scale, then, could not Judgement day actually be a time when humanity evolves spiritually, our vibration shifting to the extent that the Otherworld and its inhabitants, including the Ancestors, Angels and the Sidhe, become visible and tangible in the everyday world?

In the black and white Christian viewpoint, Angels are the agents of Heaven, and Demons are the denizens of Hell, with Faeries being trapped within the earthly realm, the halfway point. Thinking shamanically, the Sidhe provide the essential balancing third point between Angels and Demons, being a little of both. They can be considered to be the Angels of the inner Earth. Whatever the cosmic truth may be, on a more 'human' level, there is a sense of sadness and shadow about the Sidhe, which goes hand in hand with their light.

One of the oldest reliable accounts we have of Faery contact is that of the Reverend Robert Kirk, who himself was reputedly taken into Faery and remains there still. In *The Secret Commonwealth* he describes the nature of the Sidhe as being *"...of a middle nature betwixt man and angel."* He also notes that there is a deep sadness in their nature, and refers back to the tale of the Fall;

> *"Some say their continual sadness is because of their pendulous state, as uncertain what at the last revolution will become of them."*

This same sadness can still be keenly felt when dealing with the Sidhe today and it is somehow a fundamental part of their being. One of the most poignant portrayals of the Faery race in modern myth can be seen in Tolkien's elves. In *Fellowship of the Ring*, it is the simple hobbit gardener Sam Gamgee who captures their nature so succinctly when he says, *"They were quite different from what I expected - so old and young, and so gay and sad, as it were."* In every case when we look at the cause of this sadness, it is mysterious yet always seems to be tied in to this idea of an original home from which they have somehow been separated. As mentioned earlier this could be harking back to when they walked the surface of the Earth as we do, but perhaps this sadness reaches even further back. There is no way to truly know and who knows if even they remember, except perhaps for the span of a starlit song.

My own role with the Sidhe has been very much one of a creative mediator and I have been aware of their presence as long as I can remember even going on missions for them in my dreams! I painted the Tarot of the Sidhe through their direct inspiration and in their service and I have also been moved to bring their words through into this world. I have sung to them in the woods and heard, on one fleeting yet joyous occasion, their ethereal chorus of voices sing in return. I find it difficult to put my finger on exactly what the connection is, but I certainly feel that their energies are not so dissimilar from that of the Angels. It is no more possible to prove the origins of the Sidhe than it is to prove their existence, but I wonder who of those who love them would need or even desire any kind of conclusive proof? Their realm is fluid, and ever changing, and to know them you must not *'know'* but *'feel.'* I have felt their sadness and their joy and whatever their nature is, there is certainly something essentially *'heavenly'* about this race of magical beings. In conclusion, I would like to share with you some lyrics to a song that came through one sunny spring day...

Song of the Sidhe
Deep as the sea, we sing
As high as the Moon, we sing!
Dreaming of golden skies,
We try to forget your lies

As old as the hills,
As young as the rain,
We sing through the joy,
And dance through the pain

In twilight we dwell, unseen
Destined to live in between!
An echo is all that you hear,
A breath as we draw so near
Look for the light in the hills,
Our song can be heard there still...

A whispering wind,
A shivering leaf,
Below the above and above the beneath

As old as the sky,
As young as the day,
Endlessly wise,
But losing the way

Children of Gods, we know
The paths you have trod, we know!
Longing to breathe once more,
The cool air of your blessed shore

As old as the hills,
As young as the rain,
We sing through the joy,
And dance through the pain...

Bibliography
Evans-Wentz, W.Y.; *The Fairy Faith in Celtic Countries*; 1994; Citadel Press; USA
Kirk, Rev. Robert; *The Secret Commonwealth*; 2008; Dover Publications
Matthews, John; *The Sidhe: Wisdom from the Celtic Otherworld*; 2004; Lorian Press; Washington
Stewart, R.J.; *The Well of Light*; 2003; R.J. Stewart Books
Tolkien, J.R.R.; *The Fellowship of the Ring*; 2003; Houghton Mifflin

The Green Butterfly

Treasure-Hunting Animals, Astaroth, and King Solomon in Hiding

By Dan Harms

My first encounter with *The Green Butterfly* came through Arthur Edward Waite's *Book of Ceremonial Magic*. Waite placed this work among derivatives of the more famous *Black Pullet* that he viewed as *"quite unserious publications, which can scarcely be called spurious, as they are almost without pretence."* I know that Waite's dismissal only increased my own curiosity on this topic, and I am certain that it affected other readers in a similar matter.

The Green Butterfly, originally entitled *Grand Cabale de Papillon Vert,* is published with the infamous grimoire the *Grimorium Verum.* It does not appear in the original *Grimorium,* said to have been published *"in the ruins of Memphis"* by '*Alibeck*' in '*1517*'. Instead, the first documented appearance is in the Blocquel edition, circa 1830. After that, it appeared in the Italian editions of Bestetti (1868) and Muzzi (1880), as well as more recent editions. Joseph Peterson has recently published an English translation in his edition of the *Grimorium Verum,* along with the French and Italian texts thereof.

The *Green Butterfly* begins with a brief description of the treatise's supposed history. A magician provided a locked diamond box to the Egyptian king Sesac, telling him wait a year before unlocking it. Sesac died in battle, and the key vanished. Unable to open it, his wife gave it to the Emperor of China.

Much later, a Jewish man working for the Emperor stole it and returned it to Europe. Upon opening it, he found the document documenting the mystery of the Green Butterfly.

Our anonymous author then describes how the Green Butterfly is to be captured. Just before noon between May and July, the magician must enter a local patch of wood carrying a large butterfly net with flowers around the rim, a copper pan, and an unused snuffbox. He climbs the tallest tree in the forest and beats on a copper pan. When a flight of green butterflies appear, the largest must be snared in the net and imprisoned in the snuffbox.

Returning from the wood, the magician should place the box in the ashes from a brandy-fed fire of alder wood for thirty-eight hours. The alder wood might be significant here as a tree connected with the fairies, thus possessing a folkloric resonance to the supernatural. Next, he places the box on a church's altar under the tallest candelabrum, where it remains as the magician partakes of confession and Mass. (Given that a snuffbox under a candelabrum would likely be noticed, we can assume that the operation calls upon the assistance of a complicit priest.) The magician then waits until midnight on his saint's feast day – or, according to one edition, any day. At that time, he locks the door to his room and speaks an incantation, causing the demon Astaroth to appear.

No doubt several questions have come to mind when reading this description. I will give the best answers I can for them, while realizing that much still remains to be explained here.

Who is Sesac, and why is he important? The book's supposed chain of transmission, emphasizing exotic locations (Egypt, China) and individuals (the unnamed Jew), is a common feature of grimoires. Works such as the *Sefer Raziel* and the *Key of Solomon* often include a bewildering number of owners, passing from remote antiquity through the leading lights of religious tradition to the lucky reader. Unique to the *Green Butterfly* is the mention of Sesac, King of Egypt, most likely identifiable as the pharaoh Shoshenq I. Sesac is mentioned twice in the Bible (*1 Kings 14:25, 2 Chronicles 12:1-12*) as the king who conquered Jerusalem and bore off the treasures of Solomon's temple. We should not ignore the magician from whom Sesac obtains the box, but the title *'Cabala'* suggests that the book was intended to have a Hebrew origin. Could it be that a previous edition linked the Green Butterfly operation with King Solomon, considered the most powerful magician of antiquity, and that this became garbled later with the story of the necromancer?

What is the green butterfly? Is it natural or supernatural? Out of the species depicted in the *Collins Butterfly Guide*, the olive skipper (*Pyrgus serratulae*) seems the most likely candidate. It is almost entirely green, it appears through most of France from mid-May to July, and it appears in clearings in forests. I will leave it to the entomologists to wrangle over this identification.

Nevertheless, let us consider the other possibility: that the butterfly is a supernatural being. The first temptation is to associate the butterfly with the fairy realm. Indeed, Katherine Briggs tells us that the eighteenth century was the first time that butterfly-winged fairies became popular. In addition, the flowers of the alder are used to make green dye, the same coloration as the traditional garb of the fairies. The evidence remains circumstantial, as no explicit elements of fairies appear in the ritual.

The content of the rite might point us in a different direction. When the magician comes into the woods, he is urged to say the *"Oration of the Salamanders."* This prayer, originally derived from the comic novel *Le Comte de Gabalis* (1670), appeared later in both the *Grimorium Verum* and the *Black Pullet*. Could it be that the butterfly in this scene is considered to be an elemental spirit of fire? The warm weather in which the ritual takes place might also indicate this.

Who is Astaroth? Astaroth is a derivation of the goddess Astarte, who was worshiped from Mesopotamia to Phoenicia to Egypt. She was the deity whose worship Solomon pursued and to whom he built a high place on the Hill of Corruption (*1 Kings 11, 2 Kings 23:13*), once again bringing us back to the Biblical king. Though some scholars have connected Astarte with fertility or love, this attribution might be due to the proscriptive attitude of the Biblical scribes against foreign and religious sexuality. Her portfolio, when it is stated, seems to be that of a goddess of battle.

Astaroth's role in the Old Testament was the impetus bringing her into the demonic pantheon of the Christian era. She had a brief stay on the side of the angels, as the angel Asteraoth in the *Testament of Solomon* is depicted as warding off the evil spirit of Power. Nonetheless, by the time of the *Green Butterfly*, Astaroth was clearly male and one of the demonic forces.

We might ask whether the demon Astaroth, as portrayed in grimoires, reflects the amatory nature that early Christians associated with the goddess. As it turns out, Astaroth does appear in some incantations for love found in these books. For example, the Munich handbook published n *Forbidden Rites* provides a spell to create an image of the beloved, to which Belial, Astaroth, and Paymon are called to make it effective. The recently-published *Collection of Magical Secrets* includes a rite in which the name 'Astoroth' is pricked three times into a piece of fruit with a needle and then given to the intended.

Overall, however, Astaroth seems to have become a popular demon of general aspect, useful for a wide range of purposes. In the *Lemegeton*, he appears as *"an unbeautiful angel, ridding on an Infernall like dragon"* (Peterson 20), and knows every secret, the liberal sciences, and why the fallen angels were cast out.

Other experiments in the Munich handbook call upon him to appear in a child's thumbnail in a divinatory rite or to bring hatred between two people. E. M. Butler's *Ritual Magic* mentions a ritual calling upon Astaroth to drive off a poltergeist in the *Magia naturalis et innaturalis* attributed to Faust.

By the time of the *Green Butterfly*, Astaroth was very much part of the French occult scene. Numerous reports had circulated as to how, during the 17th century Affair of the Poisoners, Madame de Montespan called out to Astaroth and Asmodai to bring her the king's favour during Black Masses at which infants were sacrificed. The popular magical works of that time and place also featured Astaroth in a prominent role. The *Grimoire of Honorius* hailed him as one of the seven demons attributed to the days of the week, while the *Grand Grimoire* lists him as the intermediary between the supreme devil Lucifer and Lucifuge Rofocale, with whom the magician creates a pact.

Astaroth also appears in the *Green Butterfly's* companion work *Grimorium Verum* as one of the three superior spirits who serves with Lucifer and Beelzebuth under the *'Emperor,'* presumably of hell (p. 11). Astaroth can appear as a donkey or human of white and black. He is seen as the spirit governing the Americas, a reflection of his assignment to the west in Greek copies of the *Key of Solomon*. The *Grimorium* provides the formulae for calling up Astaroth, but it does not state any particular purpose for doing so. Given the similarities between the hierarchies here and in the *Grand Grimoire*, we might assume that calling him is necessary to invoke the lesser spirits. Nonetheless, in the *Green Butterfly* Astaroth is not part of any hierarchy, but instead performs his numerous functions without other assistance.

Those seeking Astaroth's connections with love will find a few hints thereof in the Green Butterfly. Not only will the demon locate and introduce a future spouse to the magician, he also will lead any person to the magician's chambers - presumably for other purposes than conversation. Nonetheless, Astaroth also presents a number of other services to the magician, including invisibility, provision of wealth, instant transportation, revealing of treasure, providing favourable judgments at court, winning lotteries, and many other functions.

What does a green butterfly have to do with the demon Astaroth? This is an excellent question with no clear answer. There is a butterfly known as the Astarte fritillary (*Boloria astarte*), but it is native to the New World and not green, so we must search elsewhere.

The best solution might lie in the popular conceptions of the supernatural world, which do not make hard distinctions between the inhabitants of the supernatural realms. Angels, saints, ghosts, demons, fairies, and other spiritual entities often blend into each other in stories and legends.

If we interpret the butterfly as a fire elemental, the connection becomes even stronger. The treatise *On Nymphs, Sylphs, Pygmies and Salamanders*, attributed to Paracelsus, states:

> *"You must know, however, that there is danger with the fire people, because they are commonly possessed, and the devil thus rages in them, which causes great harm to man. (p. 240)"*

Thus, the distance between our mysterious butterfly and the demonic realm might not be as great as it initially appears.

What of Waite's statement that this work was merely a cheap derivative of *The Black Pullet*? At first, Waite's placement of the book in a sub-genre of magical works intended to create or attract a magical helper seems appropriate. The most prominent of these is *The Black Pullet*, or *Pullet Noir*, but other titles include the *Chouette Noir* (*Black Screech Owl*), *Reine des Mouches Velues* (*Queen of the Hairy Flies*), and even the curious procedure for the Hand of Glory found in the *Grimorium Verum* itself. Most of these involve the capture or breeding of a magical creature intended to aid the creator in locating treasure.

The matter is further confused by the presence of two rituals under the name of *'The Black Pullet,'* both of which Waite includes in his book. The first of these, appearing in the book known as *The Old Man of the Pyramids,* discusses the breeding of a hen which can scent out treasure. Upon closer examination, only two similarities emerge: each includes the Oration of the Salamanders as a prayer, and each seeks as a goal the revelation of buried money. Nonetheless, the Black Pullet rite includes nothing of an explicitly demonic nature, and the black chicken is only useful for finding treasure.

Waite also cites a second ritual under the Black Pullet name that has a more infernal cast. In it, the operator bears a black virgin hen to a crossroads at midnight. There, after drawing a circle with a cypress wand about him, he tears the chicken in half and states a brief phrase, following it with the *'Grand Appellation,'* at which point a spirit appears who the magician may command to bring him treasure. The goal of the ritual seems similar, and the *'Grand Appellation'* is called for in both rites. Nonetheless, the Green Butterfly's ties to nature, the elaborate procedures surrounding it, and the lack of the Black Pullet's more grotesque aspects leave considerable space between the two. On the whole, Waite's accusation seems unfair.

This is not to say that the Green Butterfly does not bear the marks of commercialism, as parts of it have been written to require rituals from other books. The Blocquel edition's procedure requires the user to speak the *'Grand Appellation'* from the *Dragon Rouge,* yet another release from the same publisher. In addition, the ritual immediately before the treatise in the *Grimorium Verum,* intended to find one's future spouse during the nine months the Green Butterfly may not be hunted, refers to the grimoire *Enchiridion,* yet another publication from that company. (The Italian editions require the prayer *De Profundis* instead.) This need not mean, however, that the Green Butterfly was created to expand the publisher's purse. For example, when the De Laurence Company of Chicago released the *Key of Solomon* in the early 20th century, they inserted at least one advertisement for their products into the main text.

The ending of the Green Butterfly leaves us with many unanswered questions. What does the butterfly have to do with the demon? Is Astaroth's service to the magician only for the time when called, or is there an ongoing relationship? What if the snuffbox were to be stolen or opened? If there are answers, the present text does not indicate them. It might be that other editions of this work, discovered in other printed works or in the manuscript tradition, will illuminate these questions.

UPDATE: Before this article went to press, I received a copy of Jake Stratton-Kent's fine *True Grimoire* (Scarlet Imprint, 2009). Though there is much to admire in the book, my examination of the *Green Butterfly*, *Black Pullet*, *Black-Screech-Owl*, and *Queen of the Hairy Flies* shows little to support his hypothesis that the four rites are geared toward the four elements.

THE FALLEN ANGELS AND THE GOETIA
David Rankine

"Tu operans sis secretus horum"[18]

The Goetia is the first of the five books which together constitute the grimoire known as the *Lemegeton*. Although the earliest extant *Lemegeton* dates to 1641 (Sloane MS 3825), its roots can be traced through the preceding centuries. The earliest of these is probably the small fifteenth century French grimoire, *Le Livre des Espiritez* (Trinity MS 0.8.29) which lists forty-seven demons, with more than thirty of them appearing in the *Goetia*. Another fifteenth century manuscript which names a large number of spirits is the Latin text, *Codex Latinus Monacensis 849* (CLM 849). This text has less overlap, with twenty or so of the spirit names (or variations) found in the *Goetia*. However this text does demonstrate the prevalence of many of the Goetic spirits in the preceding centuries before their coalescence into the *Goetia*.

The German religious scholar-magician Abbot Johannes Trithemius mentioned a manuscript called *Composition of the Names and Characters of the Evil Spirits* in his work *Antipalus* (1508). This manuscript has been lost, but from the title it seems a likely source for the names and seals of the seventy-two Evil Spirits in the *Goetia*. As Dr Thomas Rudd's copy of the *Lemegeton* (1656) begins with the title of *Liber Malorum Spirituum* ('*Book of Evil Spirits*'), this connection does seem

---

18 "Thou that works them, be secret in them."

likely. If this is the case, then the *Goetia* already existed before 1508, in Trithemius' possession, though we cannot say where the Abbot got his copy from.

The manuscript Sloane MS 3824 (1649), contains a unique mixture of material, including an invocation of the triumvirate of Lucifer, Beelzebub and Sathan, as rulers of the demons. This invocation is a pre-conjuration directing the demon rulers to direct their spirits, who will be summoned by the magician, to perform his will. This manuscript contains a mixture of material which can be described as proto-Goetic, including the use of some of the Goetic spirits for revealing treasure trove,[19] a spirit contract of Padiel, conjurations of the Wandering Princes, and an English translation of some of Abbot Johannes Trithemius' *Steganographia*, which would form part of the *Theurgia-Goetia*.

In this manuscript it is significant that these powerful fallen spirits are fulfilling a divinely appointed role:

> "O All you Spirits of great power L:B:S:[20] unto whom By Orders & Offices, as Messengers of wrath, & Ministers of divine Justice, the Execution of God's Judgement are committed, & accordingly at his Commandment by you fulfilled, on all sublunar things, Creatures & places whatsoever & wheresoever he shall decree and appoint the same to be inflicted."[21]

Here we must ask the question of *"did they fall or were they pushed?"* By this I mean that it was a common view that many (or indeed all) of the fallen angels were fulfilling the divine will. This would then mean that they had to fall to fulfil their roles as rulers of the infernal hierarchy. This view is one which caused many people to be burned as heretics, such as the Cathars who worshipped Lucifer by the name of Lucibel (*'beautiful light'*), and considered him to be the son of God who

---

19 See The Book of Treasure Spirits, Rankine, 2009.
20 This contraction "L:B:S:" refers to Lucifer, Beelzebub and Sathan. These three are part of the hierarchy implied but not included in the Lemegeton.
21 Sloane MS 3824.

rebelled. From the Cathars, he was soon referred to in the French witch trials, such as that of Prous Boneta in 1325, and denigrated to rebel without a cause. To the grimoire magician conjuring spirits from the Goetia and other texts, his cause was laid out by God, and so Lucifer's role was arguably one of the most important in the whole demonic hierarchy.

Amaymon is another powerful spirit referred to in the *Goetia*, though not as one of the seventy-two spirits. He is the demon king of the South or East depending on which grimoire you are using (*Le Livre des Espiritez*, the *Key of Solomon*, Agrippa and conjurations of the king of the direction in Sloane MS 3821 and Rawlinson MS D1363 all give the south, whereas the *Goetia* has east as his direction).

One of the most noteworthy phenomena in the *Goetia* is the number of spirits who are described as fallen angels. By direct statement or implication, nineteen of the Goetic spirits can be clearly labelled as fallen angels, with four hoping to be restored to grace within 1200 years. Amongst these spirits, six of the nine orders of angels are mentioned, either as their origins, or the origins of the spirits they rule. The orders which are described as the origins of the Goetic spirits are the Seraphim, Thrones, Dominations, Potestates or Powers, Virtues, and Angels. The orders which are absent are as significant as those which are included, in that none of the spirits are said to come from the Cherubim, Principalities or Archangels.

One of the major spirits of the *Goetia* is Belial (68).[22] Belial is described as belonging to the same angelic order as Lucifer, i.e. he is of the Seraphim, and that he was created next after Lucifer. Belial declares he fell in the first and greatest of the falls when the angels fought. Unlike all the other Goetic spirits, Belial demands sacrifices. He rules eighty legions, which are drawn from the orders of Virtues and of Angels. Belial is also

---

22 The number in brackets represents the position in the sequence of the 72 Goetic spirits.

found in the *Abramelin* as one of the four superior spirits (along with Lucifer, Leviathan and Satan), and is described as the Prince and Ruler of the third of the nine orders of demons, the Vessels of Iniquity.[23]

There are three spirits from the order of Virtues, all of whom are particularly linked with treasure, these being Agares (2), Barbatos (8) and Vassago (3). Vassago is not actually named as being an angel, but he is described as being of the same nature as Agares, implying this is the case. Barbatos is described in the *Goetia* as breaking open hidden treasures laid by the enchantment of magicians. All three of these spirits are listed as treasure spirits for obtaining treasure trove in Sloane MS 3824.

Agares and Vassago are two of the spirits mentioned in connection with the English King, Edward IV (reigned 1461-83). Ebenezer Sibley and Frederick Hockley both reproduced *"An Experiment of me J.W. with the Spirits Birto, Agares, Balphares & Vassago as hath often been proved at the instant request of Edward the Fourth King of England."*[24] Whilst the idea of Goetic conjurations being performed for an English monarch is extremely appealing, it is clear from the images and wording that this is material derived from Sloane MS 3824. In that manuscript, which is around two hundred years older, the experiments of spirits are all described, but only Birto is described in relation to the king. The heading is significantly different but also recognisably the source of the Sibley reference, and reads, *"An Experiment of the Spirit Birto as hath often been proved at the instant request of Edward the Fourth King of England."* This is much more plausible, as there are no known manuscripts of the *Goetia* prior to 1641, the date of Sloane MS 3825, which is the earliest extant *Lemegeton*.[25]

---

23 See The Keys to the Gateway of Magic, Skinner & Rankine, 2005, for more information.
24 See e.g. Wellcome MS 3203, John Rylands GB 0133 Eng MS 40.
25 Reproduced in The Lesser Key of Solomon, Peterson, 2001.

Barbatos is identified with Barbason, the name of a treasure spirit associated with Vassago and Agares and other treasure spirits in Sloane MS 3824. Barbason seems to first occur in Shakespeare's writings, in *The Merry Wives of Windsor*, in the line *"I am not Barbason, you cannot conjure me"* and also in the line *"Amaimon founds well; Lucifer, well; Barbason well; yet they are devils' additions."*[26] In the notes to the play in a 1790 version, George Steevens made the identification of Barbatos with Barbason, quoting Scott's version of *Pseudomonarchia Daemonum* as his source, although Barbason is not actually there.

Two spirits are definitely from the order of Dominations, Paimon or Paymon (9) and Marchosias (35). A third spirit, Balam (51), although he is not described as being angelic in the *Goetia*, is described as such in Johannes Weyer's *Pseudomonarchia Daemonum*, the main source of the *Goetia*. Weyer's description is nearly identical word for word to that subsequently used in the Goetia, with the addition of the phrase *"and was of the order of Dominations"*[27] at the end.

Paimon is described in other grimoires as the King of the West, i.e. as one of the four demon kings of the directions, hence the description that he is to be observed towards the West. As well as being an angel himself, Paimon also governs one hundred legions of spirits from the order of Angels and another hundred legions of spirits from the order of Potestates. That Paimon is one of the most powerful of the Goetic spirits is also demonstrated by the fact that the magician is instructed to make an offering to him.

Marchosias is the first of the angels who told Solomon they hoped to return to the seventh throne after 1200 years. As Solomon lived far more than 1200 years before the first known copy of the *Goetia*, we have to make one of several assumptions.

---

26 Shakespeare also refers to Amaimon and Lucifer in King Henry IV.
27 Pseudomonarchia Daemonum, Weyer, 1563.

These are that either (a) the magician recording the information made a mistake, or (b) these spirits may no longer be available, having gone back to full angel status, or (c) God was not in a forgiving mood. The latter option is perhaps indicated by Weyer in *Pseudomonarchia Daemonum*, in his description of Amy, also called Auns (58). Weyer gives angelic roots to Amy, saying, *"He is partly of the order of Angels, partly of Potestates, he hopes after a thousand two hundred years to return to the seventh throne, which is not credible."*[28]

Several other spirits, who are not specifically named in connection with any of the orders, are also described as hoping to return to the seventh throne after 1200 years. These are Phenix or Phoenix (37) and probably Shax (44). I say probably, because Shax is described as stealing money out of king's houses and returning it after 1200 years (in both *Pseudomonarchia Daemonum*, and the *Goetia*). This seems more likely to be a copyist's error, with a line referring to hopes of returning to the seventh throne omitted, resulting in this bizarre suggestion of returning money after so many centuries. This then of course raises the question of where Weyer was copying his list of demons from! Forcalor (41) has a shorter sentence, hoping to return to the seventh throne after 1000 years.

Four of the spirits are described as coming from the order of Potestates, which is sometimes called the order of Powers, the translation of the name. These spirits are Beleth or Bileth (13), Gaap (33), Vuall (47), and Crocell or Procell (49). Bileth is unique in that he is the only Goetic spirit whose description includes instructions for the use of the hazel wand. The magician is instructed to command Bileth into the triangle in the South-East with the wand. Additionally the magician is instructed to have a silver ring on the middle finger of his left hand held against his face, as is instructed for Amaymon. Reference is made in the section entitled *Observations* about

---

28 Pseudomonarchia Daemonum, Weyer, 1563.

Solomon's magical ring, which is to be held before the face of the exorcist to preserve him from fumes, and Johannes Weyer in his description of Astaroth in *Pseudomonarchia Daemonum* states it should be made of silver. Referring to the stinking breath of Astaroth, Weyer wrote *"And therefore let the conjuror hold near to his face a magical silver ring, and that shall defend him."*[29]

The intriguing reference to the use of the ring *'as is instructed for Amaymon'* suggests lost information, as Amaymon is not one of the seventy-two Goetic spirits (he is the King of the East or South), rather he is called in the Invocation of the King before the general curse known as the spirit's chain used on recalcitrant spirits (who are in the dominion of the East, such as Asmodai, Gaap and Seer). Bileth may be derived from Bilet, one of the angels of the air ruling Monday in the Heptameron.

Gaap has some interesting qualities, being able to instruct the magician how to consecrate things that belong to the domination of Amaymon, and also to deliver other magician's familiars to the conjuring magician. Gaap is also described as one of the four chiefs (with Bileth, Asmodai and Belial) of the spirits commanded into the brass vessel by Solomon. Gaap is also described in the section entitled Observations as the king ruling the south, which fits with the description that he appears when the sun is in some of the southern signs.

Vuall could be a useful spirit for anyone interested in ancient Egypt, as he is described as being able to speak in the Egyptian tongue, but not perfectly! His entry also provides the snippet of information that a legion contains 6666 spirits. Procell specifically appears in the form of an angel, rather than any of the animalistic or anthropomorphic forms worn by many of the other Goetic spirits.

One spirit, Camio or Caim (53) is from the order of Angels, and one spirit is from the order of Thrones, the only Superior

---

29 Pseudomonarchia Daemonum, Weyer, 1563.

Hierarchy angel in the whole Goetia, and that is Raum (40). However two spirits Alloces (52) and Murmus or Murmur (54) are uniquely described as being partly of the order of Thrones and partly of the order of Angels. This cross-order combination is not seen for any of the other Goetic spirits, with the exception of Amy in Weyer's description, and only occurs elsewhere in describing their servant spirits as being from two different angelic orders. Therefore this is something of an anomaly, that angels should belong to two separate orders in this manner.

The remaining two spirits I have included are not named as belonging to any of the Angelic orders, but rule spirits from two orders each. Purson (20) is described as ruling spirits from the orders of Virtues and Thrones, Forners or Forneus (30) rules spirits from the orders of Angels and Thrones. The orders are from the three ranks of angelic hierarchies, i.e. the Thrones from the Superior Hierarchy, the Virtues from the Middle Hierarchy, and the Angels from the Inferior Hierarchy. Finally I should also mention the spirit who was left behind in the *Pseudomonarchia Daemonum* and did not get included in the *Goetia*. He is Pruflas or Bufas, whose abode is around the Tower of Babylon, where he is seen like a flame outside. He has twenty-six legions, partly from the order of thrones, and partly from the order of Angels.

So bearing in mind that over a quarter of the spirits in the Goetia are fallen angels by description or implication, the question that has to be asked in ending this discussion of the fallen angels and the *Goetia* is: is that also true for others of them and we just haven't found the evidence or accepted the idea yet?

Bibliography – MSS
Codex Latinus Monacensis 849
Harley MS 6483
Rawlinson MS D1363
Sloane MS 3821
Sloane MS 3824
Sloane MS 3825
Trinity MS 0.8.29

Bibliography – Printed Sources
Butler, E.M.; *Ritual Magic*; 1949; Cambridge University Press; Cambridge
Kieckhefer, Richard; *Forbidden Rites: A Necromancer's Manual of the Fifteenth Century*; 1997; Sutton Publishing Ltd; Stroud
Peterson, Joseph H. (ed); *The Lesser Key of Solomon*; 2001; Wieser Books; Maine
Rankine, David (ed); *The Book of Treasure Spirits*; 2009; Avalonia; London
Shakespeare, William; *The Plays and Poems of William Shakespeare* Volume 1 Part 2; 1790; H. Baldwin; London
Skinner, Stephen, & Rankine, David; *The Goetia of Dr Rudd*; 2007; Golden Hoard Press; Singapore
Skinner, Stephen, & Rankine, David; *The Keys to the Gateway of Magic*; 2005; Golden Hoard Press; Singapore

FIGURE TO BE ENGRAVED ON THE MAGICIAN'S RING FROM WAITE'S BOOK OF CEREMONIAL MAGIC

DEMONS AND DEVILS
By Maestro Nestor

Since grimoire magic deals mostly with the art of commanding demons and devils it is of course a prerequisite to learn about them if you are interested in the grimoires. I approach this subject from a traditional western mysticism angle, concentrating on the demons and devils from a Jewish, Christian or Arabic belief. Religion play an important role in grimoire work and it is in the religions we find most of the information about the origins and theory about demons and devils. A tip is to read as many as possible of the religious titles I have included in the bibliography. Religion really does hold a lot of keys to this kind of magic, and it is important to remember that many of those who wrote and worked with the grimoires were priests or truly believed in the religion. First it is worth considering the history of demons' origins and possible explanations on how they work. After that I discuss what I call the inner and outer demons. This is a heated and much debated topic between the traditional grimoire workers and modern practitioners.

History

Belief in demons has existed since we have had a written language and probably back to the early beginnings of humanity. Most religions have demons in their mythology. Sometimes they are not called demons but share the same qualities as a demon does. For example the Arabs refer to djinns, but upon closer examination it is clear that djinns and demons are really the same thing. Since most of the grimoires we are talking about have either a Christian or Jewish background (with the exception of the *Picatrix*) we will mainly look at those two belief systems mythology about demons.

The most popular theory on demons is that they were cast down from heaven by God after an uproar led by Lucifer[30] with help by Samael[31] and Azazel.[32] These so-called fallen angels were then subsequently called demons.

Another theory based on the *Book of Enoch* gives a different perspective. In the *Book of Enoch* a type of angel watchers called the Grigori[33] were sent down to watch over the humans, but once on earth they felt lust for the daughters of men and seduced them. This led to offspring called the Nephilim.[34] God did not approve of this and it later led to the great battle in heaven where the Grigori became fallen angels and all the Nephilim were killed. Here it is postulated that the fallen angels equal devils, and the dead souls of the Nephilim equal the demons. In revenge the fallen angels taught man the secrets of such things as make up, making weapons and so on.

In Jewish demonology the demons existed before the fall of the angels. An example of this is Adam's first wife Lilith.[35] Lilith left Adam[36] after he tried to force himself on her for sex, she subsequently joined Samael and is believed to have united with him. Lilith actually comes from the Mesopotamian pantheon[37] and was later adopted into the Jewish demonology. This

---

30 Lucifer, The light giver. St. Jerome and other Church Fathers are responsible for labelling Lucifer Satan. Davidson Gustav, A Dictionary of Angels Including the fallen angels, page 176.

31 Samael, The angel of death, The Chief of the Satans, ibid, p255.

32 Azazel, Lord of hell and seducer of mankind. He "taught men to fashion swords and shields" and women "the art of beautifying the eyelids," ibid, p63.

33 Grigori, the eternally silent watchers from the secret Book of Enoch, ibid, p126-7.

34 Nephilim, The child between an angel and the daughters of men. They are said to have built the Tower of Babel, ibid, p206.

35 Lilith, the enemy of infants, Adams first wife, the mother of Cain and now the bride of Samael, ibid, p174-5.

36 Adam, The biblical figure from the book of Genesis.

37 Lilith comes from the female Mesopotamian demon ardat lili. Davidson, A Dictionary of Angels Including the fallen angels, p174.

happened with many of the old Gods and demons which the Christians and Jews encountered.

There are no clear definitions since the Church has demonised any being they considered evil. Things have been called demonic or given demonic or devilish properties for a long time by the Church to put fear in the hearts of those that oppose it, scaring their followers to obedience so they follow political goals that have nothing to do with the actual religion. This behaviour has been most common in the Catholic and Protestant Churches. A good example of this is the demonization of wolves in Europe. The attitude towards wolves differs greatly between the Catholic, Protestant countries and the Orthodox. A wolf simply isn't seen as a pure evil being in the Orthodox countries.

Satan is another character that there are many theories on. The most popular without question being that he is Lucifer. There are other theories worth mentioning though. In the *Book of Enoch* we see the word *Satans*[38] which is Satan in plural. From there came the idea that he is not one being but a combination of different beings that all act towards the same goal with Samael being the chief of the Satans. That is my favourite theory.

Demons also have levels of importance or hierarchies. At the top we find demons such as Belial, Beelzebub and Satanachia. These are probably not the ones you want to start out your experiments with but rather save for when you have more experience if you ever actually choose to take them on. Some demons are simply better left alone all together.

Are all demons evil then? Well to answer that we have to look at how the demons became demons in the religions we are talking of. When it comes to the fallen angels that were cast out of heaven they are outcasts and abandoned by god so we can at

---

38 Concept taken from The Book of Enoch.

least say that they have no support for what they are doing from god anymore. They are not bound by any of the rules a normal angel is bound by or the appropriate morals. It might not exactly make them evil but definitely unpredictable. There were though other ways to end up being a demon in these belief systems. They could have been adopted from other older belief systems like Lilith as aforementioned or they could have been gods in another belief system like the Greek, Roman or Egyptian. The religious answer to how this could occur lies in *Deuteronomy* 5:7-10:

> *"You shall have no other gods before me. You shall not make for yourself an idol, whether in the form of anything that is in heaven above, or that is on the earth beneath, or that is in the water under the earth. You shall not bow down to them or worship them; for I the Lord your God am a jealous God, punishing children for the iniquity of parents, to the third and fourth generation of those who reject me, but showing steadfast love to the thousandth generation of those who love me and keep my commandments."*

This is probably the reason why most of the things they encountered during history were labelled as demons or devils. The demons and devils in Judaism, Christianity and Islam are something that is not of God and therefore cannot be good. This is of course something that each individual needs to make up their own minds about. I only give the religious answer here.

Inner and Outer demons

I divide demons in to two different categories, the inner and outer demons. Inner demons are basically the sins you commit and what is stopping you from being pure. For those that think of the grimoires as black magic this might come as a surprise and a bit of shock but the paradox is that for you to be able to practice many of the grimoires you must be pure of heart and free of sin.

When speaking of sin, think in terms of the ten commandments, and the seven sins represented by lust, gluttony, avarice, sloth, pride, envy and anger. These are all inner demons that we need to conquer. Any weakness is a way in for an outer demon, so work first with taking care of the inner ones. I would not recommend you to do this if you're on any kind of mind altering drugs. This includes all medicines that you take for depression, beta blockers, anxiety, strong pain killers, alcohol, and illegal drugs and so on. Do not worry though, as this is what all the fasting and prayer is for. Actually there are many things designed in the grimoires to open you up to your inner divine spark and you do not have to be super holy to do this kind of magic. You do on the other hand have to be free from inner temptations.

Outer demons are the ones we are evoking during the rituals. The ones that make the magic happen and who fulfil our wishes and desires. Some magicians claim that demons are all a part of our psyche. Some do not go as far as to say straight out that it is our imagination which conjures up the images of the demons, but that it is something not far from that. I on the other hand believe in them to be separate from our minds and beings in their own right, and my beliefs of angels and Gods are the same. There is no question that your mind matter and to be able to see anything you need to reach a certain stage of mind where your divine spark is strong and clear. I have seen and experienced too much to be able to agree that it is just my mind playing tricks on.

How we can use them

Much like with God and the angels teaching Moses magic on the Sinai Mountain, the fallen angels taught Cham the secret arts of magic. So Cham and his people became the second Satanists, but the first ones who were taught from the fallen angels. Cain is in many ways the first Satanist of the Bible but he worshipped the other gods who were there before the flood of Noah, so he had no direct contact with the fallen angels, and is because of that, of less importance to us.

We can work with demons for many different reasons. Knowledge probably being one of the most accepted reasons for conjuring and calling upon a demon, but there are of course endless reasons you may wish to do so. You can get them to point you to the direction of hidden treasure, bring you love, cause hate, fight for you, heal people, kill people, make you food, transportation and the list just goes on and on. This is if you take the grimoires' claim for what they can do at face value. I will however be the first to admit that I have not tried many of those things I just listed!

I once played with the idea of summoning a lesser demon to see if I could get it to clean the apartment but later decided that it was just too disrespectful. The demons should always be treated with respect. At the same time it is also important to never forget that the demons you conjure are most certainly not your friend either. They can and they will be dangerous if you let them. This is not a game and there are many things to consider before you decide to enter the exiting world of grimoire magic.

Pact Making

Making pacts with demons of different levels is not that uncommon in Grimoire magic but it can be very dangerous and have life changing effects on you. This is why I have decided to tell you my story of a pact I made.

First of all I should probably explain a bit about my background. I was a practising Satanist for almost 5 years before I turned over to rather strictly right hand path practise and the pact was a big reason as to why I changed. The pact was obviously made during my years as a Satanist.

There are a few things I will not talk about when it comes to this pact and I have never talked to anyone else about that either. First is exactly how it was done and second is the nature of the pact. There are several reasons why I won't talk about that but none I want to share. I can however tell you quite a lot I think without explaining those two things.

As I think most are when making this kind of pact I was then in a situation of thinking my life sucked so much that it was worth a try. I think most of you will agree that it was not the best time to make any kind of deals. Anyway the deal was created for this demon to fulfil a certain amount of things I wanted and when it had fulfilled its part it could do whatever pleased it. You can say the list was of things I wanted to have done before I passed away.

The results were scary to say the least. One of the terms was fulfilled the night after the pact was done and I got what I wanted with rather amazing speed. One thing I asked for was something that would take years even with help from a demon. So I can attest that making pacts does work without a doubt.

After a few years I started to think about that pact again because I was feeling really good and my life was fulfilling. All of a sudden the thought of a demon being able to do what it wanted to with me was much less appealing. I started to explore ways to break the deal and get off. There are plenty of pact-breaking types of magic out there and I probably tried them all, but nothing worked. Then one day the pact had been fulfilled on the demon's part and I was still trying to find ways to get out.

So what happens when it's your turn to pay back then? Well for me it was tons of things. Huge depressions, sickness and no doctors could diagnose me. I went from being used to teaching computers to 300 people in a lecture room to not being able to walk outside of my own door. In 3 years I lost my grandmother on my father's side, both grandparents on my mother's side, my dad had two strokes and is still alive but not well, my mother died, some friends died and my brother turned on me. Sure all of this could have been coincidences but I doubt it.

I did find a solution though. It took a long time to find one but in the end it was rather simple. You cannot break your own pact - you have to find someone that does it for you. This was what I had been doing wrong all these years. Thanks to a very talented magician I was suddenly cleared from the pact and could live a normal life again. I still do magic but there is no way I am making another pact ever again. It is not worth it. I learned from this that through your own divine spark you can control the demons and make them do what you want to without owing them a thing. How this will affect my afterlife I am not sure, but I guess no one can know until they are there. I try to do my share of paying back though. For a long time I helped people with spiritual problems and I still do from time to time. I only approach magic from a right hand path perspective today but have still managed to keep out of organised religions. I do believe though but far from a normal believer and I do not limit myself to a single belief system.

The idea on how to rid me of the pact came from a small pact breaking ritual found in Waite's Book of Ceremonial Magic.[39] With that in mind and also the catholic exorcism found in *Rituale Romanum* the magician used a self made ritual calling out angels and gods in big numbers on the astral plane and begged them to set me free. I could actually feel it lifting about the same time as the holy beings agreed to fix it even if I was not told when it was going to happen. I was just told the week the ritual would be performed. So the demon in question that I made the pact with was never called by the magician. My guess is that the holy beings have ways to deal with things like that. Also both the magician and I felt it would be rather pointless trying to get the demon itself to back out of the deal. The demon was named in the ritual to the holy beings as was my name.

The demon I called for was Satan as I was a Satanist back then and a theist Satanist. The demon showing up I figured was Samael. It was not so smart making pacts with the former angel of death, I know that now. The only thing I can say in my

---

39 The Book of Ceremonial Magic, Waite, page 262, chapter 6 "The mysteries of infernal evocation according to the grand grimoire". The rite is from a "Manual of Exorcisms" by Abbé Eynatton published in 1678.

defence was that I was young and desperate when I made the pact.

Well I hope you all do not think I am a total nut after telling you all this and I am sure people have had different experiences with pacts. This was just my story of how it affected my life. I guess some good things came out of it in the end. I definitely learned a lot trying to get rid of the deal and ended up a lot wiser in the end. Sometimes you need to mess up totally I guess before you grow up and start to understand that things change and what you do one day might not be a good idea the next day.

If you still want to experiment with making pacts be smart and never give up more then you are willing to part from. That is probably the best advice I can give on the matter.

Warrior Ten

The Great Task

THE GREAT TASK, SIDHE TAROT, BY EMILY CARDING

GRIMOIRES FOR PAGANS
By Jake Stratton Kent

'O Thou, the apex of the plane
With ibis head and phoenix wand
And wings of night, whose serpents strain
Their bodies, bounding the beyond
Thou in the Light and in the Night
Art one above their moving might'.

Unlike a lot of ceremonial magicians who employ the grimoires, *'I don't do Angels'*. I also don't employ conjurations rehearsing the exploits of Moses and the other leaders of Israel, be they Kings or Prophets, which they accomplished through this, that or the other name of their god. I also don't threaten spirits with knives, while hoping the names of the god of love will protect me, as I prefer to be a little more consistent, not to mention a good deal more sincere, in my combination of magic with religion.

I am, for want of a better word, a pagan. While I have some intuitive or ingrained belief in a Supreme Being out there somewhere, they don't seem terribly interested in my day to day life, or anyone else's; after all, our mundane concerns must be an anti-climax after creating the Universe. Whereas other beings, which various folks have called gods, angels, daimons, fairies, ancestors etc. are a good deal more interested and accessible. In my youth I was not at all responsive to religious education, but responded passionately to mythology and ancient history. I knew, even as a child, that this was the response I was meant to have to the approved state religion of the day, but I didn't. I was also aware, and learned to keep my mouth shut about that awareness, that we weren't the only intelligent life forms in, on and around the planet. So it was with some relief, and instant recognition, that I encountered the idea of being or becoming a magician; and the existence of magical manuals. With the help and sometimes the hindrance of these manuals I became a pagan magician.

These were the good old bad old days of the Magical Revival's second wind in the early nineteen-seventies. Back then Witchcraft, Grimoires, Aleister Crowley and all the rest weren't sewn up in scrupulously separated compartments targeted at micro-niche markets supposed to have nothing in common. It was all magic, even allowing for some individual preferences for rhyming couplets or Kabbalistic Names of Power. And it was in that milieu that I encountered the idea that the spirits of the grimoires were identical with the gods of the witches. Whatever subsequent belief systems had made of these entities, some of whom evidently still had the names of pagan gods, they were still around and might prefer being approached in a fashion suited to their former status.

This is not to say that caution should be thrown to the winds, expecting every entity to be overjoyed with your pagan credentials and instantly helpful. Not at all, magic has never been like that; gods, demons, angels, whatever you call them, some of them are dangerous, ill-tempered, and tricky, just like people. Some of them are pleasant enough, but have personal peccadilloes and 'off days', just like people. Magicians are expected to handle all that with specialised knowledge and appropriate responses.

The grimoires, in case you don't know, are magical manuals with a strong Judaeo-Christian bias. They are however also direct descendents of a magical literature of another cultural background entirely. So even allowing for the unhelpful elements introduced in the course of time, they are a useful half way house to recovering the magical approaches of an era which both I and the spirits am geared to respond to. Part of the older approach, a very substantial part, is to be found in the magical papyri of the Greco-Egyptian period and the Roman period which followed it. In these we can clearly see where the grimoires got their ideas, and also see perfectly well that the same procedures worked as readily without the aforementioned bias. The strange thing about these texts is not that they involve pagan gods, which they do, but that these pagan gods do not much resemble the elegant classical statues and prettified myths of the aristocratic literati. They have in some way reverted to a much older form, closely resembling the 'grass-roots' folk religion which Classicism misrepresents.

We are then reminded that the word Homer and other early Greek writers used for the gods was *'daimones'*. This word went through several phases of interpretation: for example Iamblichus, who first delineated Theurgy in a completely pagan context, had the daimons intermediate between gods and men, with the angels and archangels being the higher ranking daimons. There were also, even in his system, a much lower form of daimon closely akin to the meaning Christian theologians gave to the word in general. None of this need concern us particularly here, as I suspect other contributors to this book will mention different aspects of the question, and the reader can in any case pursue their own researches. What matters is that there is an established historical precedent for invoking gods and conjuring spirits which is independent of – not to mention prior to - the Judaeo-Christian paradigm. It matters too that the latter is dependent on the former, so that potential adaptations of grimoire procedures are not a departure from a grand original but a return to a truer source on a higher arc.

So how do we go about adapting the grimoires to a pagan model, while keeping whatever it is we like about the grimoires? One of the things most operators like is probably the existence of a clear cut catalogue of spirits, possessing names and sigils and an indication of their powers. Another is the equally clear cut system of correspondences – itself a Greek concept originally anyway – and the way it allows rituals to be structured appropriately to the energies invoked. The latter is something a lot of the grimoires, despite listing some colours, animals and incenses for the planets, actually don't do all that well. It is notable that the *Picatrix*, drawing directly on pagan sources, modifies the language and atmosphere of rituals of different planets, which the monotheistic grimoires do not. A Solar ritual from the *Picatrix* has a *'Sunny'* atmosphere, while a ritual of the Sun from Solomonic books has a Solomonic atmosphere. A methodology that restores and develops correspondences in an appropriate fashion is likely to be close to what most pagan conjurers would require when adapting the grimoires to a pagan model.

There are various ways to go about this, and some of them are more far reaching than others. Despite the opinions of some folks to the contrary, there is not much to be obtained from inserting the names of your favourite deities here and there in rituals composed with another approach in mind. For one thing, what you respond to and what a multi-levelled family of intelligent spirits respond to have to be considered as two different things. As this is an important aspect of what I am talking about, and there may be some misunderstanding, let's put things in perspective. It is perfectly possible to fight off an *'angry ghost'* with a name or symbol possessing deeply personal value to yourself, just as effectively as a Christian might employ the name of Jesus or the sign of the cross. That doesn't mean the same name or symbol will also work as effectively in every context of ritual magic. So substitution has to be performed with care, and the family of spirits you are working with should ideally be consulted in the process. In fact the selection of the familial group is as important a part of the process as the selection of ritual elements employed.

This being the case we are looking for an appropriate pagan pantheon or part thereof, and a responsive hierarchy of spirits. With the precedents of the papyri and of a slice of Western mythology to guide us the difficulties of the former soon disappear: 'Underworld' deities such as Persephone, Hekate and Cerberus are frequently encountered in the papyri, and traces of them remain visible in the grimoires. They are eminently suitable for working with classes of spirit equally present in both. If we are dealing with Elemental spirits the four deities named by Empedocles, who after all first formulated the concept of the Four Elements, would be ideally suitable. If the planets, then the old gods of the days of the week would be a reasonable place to start; perhaps preferring Ares, Hermes, Zeus and Aphrodite to their Norse equivalents. Interestingly enough there is a group of planetary spirits in the grimoires still referred to as 'Olympic', for which such an approach would appear tailor made.

Unfortunately this does not exhaust the obstacles in the way of our objective. There is still the matter of finding a large and adaptable family or hierarchy of spirits prepared to cooperate in a systematic reworking. There is too the matter of finding an appropriate ritual format, suitable for the spirits concerned, and adaptable to whatever categories may exist among the relevant deities and spirits. The spirits of the Goetia of Solomon may look promising as a potential spirit catalogue for this project. However, although traces of an Elemental classification are visible, its original form is probably lost irretrievably. The planetary classification supposed to apply is either garbled or farcical; are we meant to believe that out of 72 'evu-ul' demons only one corresponds to Saturn? In other words, hypothetical solutions are all very well, but the magic has to work, and stop gaps will only take us so far. If we are looking for an integrated methodology that takes us the whole way we are relying not just on a good working hypothesis, but a good bit of luck besides.

Which brings me to another part of the story of how spirits are described, and magical methods adapted, with the shifting of theological fashion. Christian magic demonised the pagan gods, no doubt about it; authors from St. Augustine to John Milton make it abundantly clear. Whether or not the demons which later bore the names of pagan gods are identical with them or not, the demonising itself is a fact. However, Christianity needed magic, and as often as it tried to suppress aspects of it, it tried to adapt others. One consequence of this love-hate relationship that is seldom understood is that the darker elements of magical tradition in the Christian period frequently bear closer relation to the older forms, despite some appearances to the contrary. Or to put it more simply, angelic magic is more heavily adapted, demonic magic less so. Now understand further that the word 'goetia' and the book called the *Goetia* of Solomon are not synonymous; other grimoires as well as far older traditions of magic are also goetic. Goetia is in fact an ancient Greek term for indigenous magical traditions prior to the adoption of the word magic itself from the Persians. So it is perhaps unsurprising that goetic magic, once liberated from the association with one particular late grimoire, is a fruitful field for the restoration of pagan magic.

This is where we start to get lucky. Possibly the most notorious of the 'darker' grimoires (bearing in mind that 'dark' often meant suspiciously pagan!) is that known as the *Grimorium Verum* or *True Grimoire*. This grimoire has some astonishingly pagan qualities, virtually unique to itself. A critical example is that the conjuring procedure relies on an intermediary spirit. A great many pagan religions and magical systems of the past relied on a god who had to be invoked before the others could be reached; a feature still present in Hinduism, where Ganesha is invoked first. This is also a feature of Voodoo in its various forms, where for example Legba or Baron Samedhi is invoked before their familial Loa may be interacted with.

The same grimoire also includes in the upper reaches of its hierarchy two major characters from the pagan systems. One of its three chiefs is Astaroth, identical with Astarte or Ishtar, and closely related to figures like Hekate and Persephone. Under Astaroth, like the other chiefs, are two deputies. One of these is called Nebiros, readily identifiable through comparison with other grimoires as Cerberus. In the papyri Cerberus and Anubis were frequently identified and treated as leaders of spirits; his status in this grimoire is virtually unchanged from the papyri, not just in general terms but in detail. In the True Grimoire then we have strong echoes of the procedures and dramatis personae of ancient magic; as well as a clear cut spirit catalogue with sigils, powers and names. So far, so good, but our good fortune continues a good deal further.

Earlier on I mentioned the Seventies as a time when the Magical Revival got its second wind, and how inclusive it was. The beginnings of the Magical Revival, at least in the English speaking world, can be traced to the Golden Dawn and its offshoots. At this time too various elements of magical tradition interacted, so that essentially modern pagan magic is also derived from that source. So also is the revival of interest in the grimoires, several of which were translated or edited by members of the Golden Dawn. So we can trace the roots of modern interest in paganism and the grimoires to the same place, regardless of the fact they are now seen as separate. Although largely unsuspected at present, might there be a route towards a reconciliation of these strands in the legacy of societies like the Golden Dawn?

A major example of such untapped potential is possibly the least investigated ritual of the early revival phase of modern magic. Though the reasons for its neglect are not difficult to trace, it is nonetheless surprising. It began life as a poetic rewrite of the Neophyte ceremony of the Golden Dawn, widely acknowledged to be of cardinal importance to that system. This adaptation was crafted by Aleister Crowley, the most notorious figure in the Magical Revival, upon whom countless pages have been expended in many languages. It was crucial to his demonstration that high level magic could be practiced while living an urban existence in a modern city; and also formed a part of some of his most high profile operations of sexual magick. With all this the ritual concerned has been omitted from most compilations of Thelemic magic, and has rarely been reprinted in its entirety. Yet it is with this ritual that our good luck with the True Grimoire holds, as it provides invaluable materials for a pagan approach to grimoire magic.

The ritual in question is known as Pyramidos, and its foremost value for us lies in the ease with which the ritual and hierarchical patterns of the True Grimoire may be harmonised with its structure. Where the True Grimoire has three chiefs of spirits – Lucifer, Belzebuth and Astaroth - Pyramidos involves three gods: Tahuti, Horus-Set and Isis. The symbolism inherent in the ritual also allows for other suitable deities to be substituted for one or other of these. Even without substitutions however, these three deities have an implicit equivalence to Hermes, Hades and Persephone, a natural triad of deities for work with underworld spirits.

Each of the three gods has such an obvious relation to the three chiefs as to facilitate a swift and effective replacement of the Christian Trinity as the powers invoked in conjuration. A triangular floor plan is a feature of both rituals, further facilitating the integration of the two. In short, by means of Pyramidos we are enabled to make a 'liturgical transplant', removing what is Catholic from the goetic process of the True Grimoire, and making comprehensive and coherent pagan substitutions. The True Grimoire calls for a ritual confession, and an Egyptian style confessional rite is included in Pyramidos. Similarly a Mass is called for by the one and provided by the other. The compatibility of the two is so striking and complete that the liturgical transplant actually enhances the original. For example during the confessional phase of the ritual two wands are to be raised alternately. In the original this action accompanies the reading of a Psalm which has no rhythmic qualities. By contrast the *'Negative Confession'* from Pyramidos is in rhyme and consists of point and counterpoint, powerfully underlining this use of the wands.

From these materials then a potent if notorious grimoire is revitalised and made accessible to modern pagan magicians. Rituals from the papyri and other pre-Christian magic can also be incorporated within the same framework as readily as the grimoire materials. This effectively brings us full circle: from the early days of the modern revival to the origins of the tradition it represents in the Egypt of Greco-Roman times, and onwards to our own time. Without rejecting two-thousand years of Christian culture we can nevertheless reclaim what is our own.

Further Reading:

Betz, Hans Dieter (ed); *The Greek Magical Papyri in Translation*; 1986; University of Chicago; Chicago

Stratton-Kent, Jake; *The True Grimoire*; 2009; Scarlet Imprint

The Equinox – British Journal of Thelema VII. 9-11. Hadean Press 2009.

Angel with the Keys of Hell releasing a demon, by Albrecht Durer

THE THWARTING ANGELS
Stephen Skinner

There are two sides to Heaven, according to Christian theology, that of the angels, and that of their *'fallen'* brothers the demons. Because Michael and his angels were portrayed as triumphing over the demons, there has always been a clear implication that the angels had and have power over these demons.

In 1497 Albrecht Durer engraved a very detailed picture of an angel releasing a demon from the pit, whilst holding a chain leash securely attached to the demon's neck, demonstrating the kind of control angels were thought to have over their fallen brothers. However the concept goes back a long way and can be found in Biblical and Deutero-canonical books.

For example the *Book of Tobit* tells the story of a woman who married seven times. On the eve of each wedding a demon, Asmodeus, strangled her intended husband before the marriage could be consummated. The story gets into its stride with the latest husband making the trip to her village whilst pondering how he could avoid the same fate. On the way he meets a traveller who tells him what to do. The traveller turns out to be the angel Raphael. His advice includes the burning of the gall of a certain fish on a chafing dish of hot coals. But it is also made very clear that Raphael is the angel that 'thwarts' the demon. *Tobit 8:2-3* makes it very clear that it is the angel who bound the demon:

> *"And as he went, he remembered the words of [the angel] Raphael, and took the ashes of the perfumes, and put the heart and the liver of the fish thereupon, and made*

a smoke therewith. The which smell when the evil spirit had smelled, he fled into the utmost parts of Egypt, and the angel bound him."

This tradition of thwarting angels is in a sense a secret tradition, as the list of names of which angel thwarts which demon is only available in a few texts. The classic text is the Testament of Solomon. As Steve Ashe remarks in his introduction to his edition of *The Testament of Solomon*, *"Solomon states that he wrote his testament before his death so that the children of Israel would know the powers and shapes of the demons, and the names of the angels who have power over them."* Although this second century CE text was probably not written by the ancient Hebrew king himself, it certainly embodied an already well established tradition of demon control.

Examples of thwarting angel and demon pairs from the Testament include:

Demon bound by	Angel
Asmodeus	Raphael
Obyzouth	Raphael
Ornias	Uriel
Arotosael	Uriel
Ruax	Michael
Barsafael	Gabriel

But there are also less well known angels in this book, such as Adonael who imprisons the demons Phobothel and Rhyx Ichthuon. Although many of these angel and demon names are just mentioned in passing the procedure used was to invoke the thwarting angel before attempting to invoke the demon, thereby giving the karcist a measure of authority and hence control.

Islam spread into Egypt in the seventh century CE, and so the torch of the magical tradition was passed from the Graeco-

Egyptian world to the Byzantine Greek world. The technique of thwarting angels was passed with the texts which were the precursors of the grimoire the *Key of Solomon* grimoire. Such a text was the *Hygromanteia*. This was supposed to have been written by Solomon for the instruction of his son Rehoboam. After discoursing on the necessity of choosing the correct planetary hour and day for a magical operation, Solomon states:

> *"Know, my very dear son Roboam [sic], that one good angel and one evil demon are lords at each hour. If you want to do a good deed, adjure the good angel so that he may be an ally to you..."*

Following this is a list of all the 24 x 7 = 184 planetary hours of the week, giving the names of corresponding angels and demons for each. For example in the 13th hour of the fifth day of the week the angel Sitioēl is matched with the demon Asmōdas [Asmodeus?].

After the fall of Constantinople in 1453 to Islam, monks, scholars and magicians fled to the Latin West, primarily Venice, bringing with them magical practices which had long ago been extinguished in Western Europe by the enthusiastic churchmen.

The pairing of angels and demons also persisted, and became part of the machinery of the grimoires. We do not have to look far to find examples of the rationale for this pairing, as one manuscript puts it: *"And besides you must understand that the Devils may be forced and constrained by the good Angels, and this is because of the Grace which the one lost, and the other as yet retains."*[40]

The details of the exact procedure are however to be found in an adjoining manuscript on the same shelf[41] which gives an expanded version of the *Lemegeton*. Instead of merely giving one seal or sigil per demon, this manuscript gives 72 double seals

---

40 Harley MS 6482.
41 Harley MS 6483, published as The Goetia of Dr Rudd, Stephen Skinner & David Rankine, volume three of the Sourceworks of Ceremonial Magic, Golden Hoard, Singapore, 2007.

which link the 72 Goetic demons with the 72 corresponding Shem ha-Mephorash angels. These angels and their associated Biblical verses from *Psalms*, are used as part of the invocatory process. The technique involves creating a double sided lamen, with the angelic seal on one side and the seal of his fallen brother on the other side.

There is an intriguing reference in the section Of the Orders of Wicked Demons and of their Fall in *Janua Magica Reserata*.[42] Rudd records that in *Psalm 72:9 "Before him the inhabitants of solitude [the demons] shall bend their knees, that is, the aerial spirits shall worship him as the Cabalists do assert, and his enemies shall lick the dust."*[43] Although this refers to God, it is a short step to include God and all his angels.

The ultimate thwarting angel could be said to be Michael (*"He who is like God"*). In the Goetia one of the places into which the demon is conjured is the triangle outside the circle. In addition to the names *'Primeumaton, Anaphaxeton and Tetragrammaton'* written along the three sides of the triangle, the inscription of *'Mi-cha-el'* is found at the three corners, indicating Michael's ability to restrain the demon. It may of course be that this drawing of the triangle was just one instance, and that other angel names are used for other demons, rather than Michael being the all-purpose demon name used to constrain the spirit into giving truthful answers.

Another clear example of thwarting angels, which is often overlooked, and which appears in grimoires, and has also made its way into Golden Dawn style magic, is the opposition of the Planetary Intelligences and the Planetary Spirits, or to give them their original names, the Planetary Angels which govern the Planetary Demons. *'Intelligence'* was a word originally used for *'angel'*.

---

42 Sloane MS 3825.
43 The Keys to the Gateway of Magic, Skinner & Rankine, Golden Hoard, Singapore, 2005.

The idea of control via the hierarchy is also reflected in the demonic hierarchy. There are senior demons of such importance that they do not have an obvious thwarting angel in the grimoires such as Satan, Lucifer and Beelzebub.[44] These demons of course also have an historical and theological dimension not associated with lesser demons. Many manuscripts make it clear that these demons were not to be treated in the same manner as the hordes of demons, but rather used as governors to control their minions. In fact they are treated more with the respect accorded to the angels! Within the same text (Sloane MS 3824) there is an interesting invocation where these demons are clearly given a divine mandate to govern the four Demon Kings of the cardinal directions, who in turn control the lesser demons.

> *"O ye Spirits & Devils, Sathan, Lucifer, Beelzebub & Dansiation; I conjure you all by your powers & strengths you are permitted to have, by Almighty God the Father, the Son & the Holy Ghost, three persons & one God, in Trinity & unity, that you enforce these 4 Kings of the 4 Gates of the World, that is Urinus or Oriens King of the East, Paymon King of the West, Amaymon King of the South, & Egin King of the North"*[45]

Although thwarting angels have a major role, it should be remembered that senior ruling demons also have a major role to play. In both instances what is significant is the hierarchy, and determining the mechanics of this chain of command is one of the keys to ensuring successful results.

Bibliography - MSS
Harley MS 6482
Harley MS 6483
Sloane MS 3821
Sloane MS 3824
Sloane MS 3825

---

44 For example Satan, although it is said that he was bound by an angel in Revelations 20, which tradition suggests is Michael. This ties in with his use in the triangle.
45 Sloane MS 3824.

Bibliography – Printed Sources

Ashe, Steven (ed); *The Testament of Solomon & The Wisdom of Solomon*; 2008; Glastonbury Books; Glastonbury

Betz, Hans Dieter (ed); *The Greek Magical Papyri in Translation*; 1996; University of Chicago Press; Chicago

Dehn, George (ed); *The Book of Abramelin*; 2006; Ibis Press; Florida

Peterson, Joseph (ed); *The Sixth & Seventh Books of Moses*; 2008; Ibis Press; Florida

Scholem, Gershom; *Major Trends in Jewish Mysticism*; 1974; Schocken Books

Skinner, Stephen (ed); *The Fourth Book of Occult Philosophy*; 1978; Askin Publishers; London

Skinner, Stephen & Rankine, David; *The Goetia of Dr Rudd*; 2007; Golden Hoard Press; Singapore

Skinner, Stephen & Rankine, David; *The Keys to the Gateway of Magic*; 2005; Golden Hoard Press; Singapore

Thompson, R. Campbell; *Semitic Magic, Its Origin and Development*; 2000; Samuel Weiser Inc; Maine

LOVING LILITH
By Melissa Harrington

Lilith is not a fallen angel, so it could be argued that she has no place in this book. However, Lilith is so steeped in the mythology of the fall, so ubiquitous in the dark fiery realms of the fallen that she cannot be ignored in an anthology such as this. Lilith has flown through the nightmares, desires and unspoken guilt of the patriarchal psyche for millennia, haunting the dreams of those who would bind her, yet desire her still, and those who fear what she might bring. She is the ultimate seductress, credited even with seducing Eve as the serpent in the Garden of Eden. Wife of Samael, and sometimes Asmodeus, she a fitting female counterpart to Lucifer, and as such has become the ultimate female deity of the left hand path.

However, Lilith also has a softer side; fully fledged she has a job to do like any fallen angel, and can be repelled by appropriate modesty, and charms. In modern times she has lent a helping hand to women finding themselves and their power within, and become a feminist and occult icon in her own right. She is an important figure in esoteric spirituality, and her study is rewarding for all those who seek her story.

From the dust of ancient deserts to Dr Who, the dark face of the feminine.

The history of Lilith shimmers like a desert mirage, leading the traveller on a meandering route through a very varied mythology. Her story seemingly begins in the desert storms of Mesopotamia, where Lil, winged demons associated with the winds of ancient Sumer, brought disease and death. She morphed out of that desert sand, her name emerging as she took form, absorbing Lailah, the Arabic night, and the Assyrian Lilitu birds with their feet, wings and talons. She merges with the demi-goddess Lamashtu in Syria.

Her most famous mythology comes from the *Alphabet of Ben Sira*, possibly a Hebrew parody, which establishes her as the first wife of Adam. Some accounts have her made from pure fire, whilst Adam is made from dirt; others have her formed of dirt while Adam is formed of dust. Whatever their provenance they are not compatible as Adam asserts his dominance by demanding she submit to lie beneath him, and she refuses, learns the magic name of God, frees herself, and flies up and flees to the desert by the red sea. The angels Senoy, Sansenoy and Semangelof are sent to fetch her back, but find her giving birth in a cave, and refusing to return. So God strikes dead 100 of her offspring a day and makes Adam another wife, this time formed of his own body. Thus it is war, and she comes to Adam in his sleep, bestrides him to rob his seed to bear more children, creating the monstrous Lilim demons, and goes in the night to destroy the children of Adam and Eve, although not taking those who are protected by amulets bearing the names Senoy, Sansenoy and Semangelof.

The Sumerian terracotta relief know as the Burney relief is thought to be the first known depiction of Lilith, and believed to date back to circa 1950 BC. She appears as the dark, destructive feminine Other throughout history; linked with the maid of desolation in the *Epic of Gilgamesh*, the night monster in Isaiah 34:14, the killer in the *Testament of Solomon*. The Talmud has references showing her as a succubus, whilst the Babylonian '*Nippur bowls*' bear incantations against Lilith as a predator to women in childbirth. Her legend grew in the *Zohar*, and the Hebrew amuletic tradition where amulets were placed over the bed or on four walls of rooms to protect women and babies from her, continuing into 18th and 19th centuries in Palestine, Persia, Morocco, Afghanistan and Kurdistan.

THE "BURNEY RELIEF" THOUGHT TO DEPICT LILLITH

She bears the epithet *'the beautiful maiden'* and is associated with prostitutes and seductive women. She has long free hair, symbol of feminine power and virility which is often red in a sign of her lust. She is powerfully beautiful, proud, and deadly. Everywhere seems to hold glimpses of her from the Dead Sea scrolls to the vampiric strix of Roman legend, and the Lamia of Greek mythology, then on into German folklore, the poems and paintings of the pre Raphaelites to the banners of the feminists, and through Angelina Jolie's CGI depiction of Beowulf's mother to children's television today; where she took pride of place with the 10th Dr Who as a powerful alien who could be young and beautiful, or old and deadly, and with her sisters, inspired Shakespeare to write 'the Scottish play'.

The Fallen

Lilith is not a Watcher, nor a Nephilim, yet she shares characteristics, functions and fate with these unearthly rebels. The *Book of Enoch* tells the story of how Shemyaza descended to earth with a gang of two hundred Watchers to fulfil his lust for the daughters of men. These earthly women happily married the angels, and were taught by them the secrets of magic in the form of incantation, divination and sorcery. They lived contentedly together, but, like Lilith, brought forth monsters with unnatural appetites. These were giants who ate all that man could produce until the mankind cried out to heaven. God prepared for the flood to cleanse the earth, and sent the Arch-Angels to bind the fallen angels, setting them to watch the slaughter of their children. The renegade angels themselves were to be thrown down for seventy generations, consumed by the fires of judgement day, and then burn forever.

The story of the fall from grace of Lucifer, and his banishment from heaven by God, is another story of pride and disobedience. Lucifer and Lilith were punished for pride, the Enochian Watchers for lust, and its consequences. Pride and lust, two shared deadly sins, with very, very deadly consequences when mixed with disobedience to God.

And yet the paradox is that they must have had a place in the scheme of things, for all powerful God created them all, and allowed this to happen. In the universe of which He is the supreme ruler Lilith found his name of power and uttered it to fly free, just as the Watchers were able to teach heavenly secrets to the children of Eve. The Lilith/Samael/serpent even becomes the guardian of the tree of knowledge who offers Eve the apple. These dark entities have rebelled against the iron Word of God and seek to teach mankind the secrets of magic, and offer them knowledge and eternal life. Like Prometheus they steal fire from

Heaven with terrible consequences for themselves, and any who would seek to make contact. Moreover, as Lilith is the mirror for all dark, repressed, magical and sexual feminine Otherness so she is the Witch, the teacher of the Dark arts, the seducer from the path of righteousness, and the holder of the keys to the forbidden secrets of the occult, the hidden truth. Thus she has come to take her place in the hearts of those who seek this path of knowledge, and dare to do so. It is not surprising that Lilith has come to be the Queen of dark magic, taking her place in its pantheon in the Fallen.

Finding the light in the darkness

So who, now, is Lilith? Is she a malign force that could cause death in childbirth? Contemporary magicians do not believe so, no more than they believe mental illness is caused by demonic possession, or that their Yule presents are brought down the chimney by Father Christmas. Today's magicians have lost the superstition and mystification that went with magic and primitive monotheism, but reclaimed the enchantment of the magical world view. They follow the laws of magic as a form of natural science, combine it with all they know of modern science, medicine, psychology, sociology, religion and any other sphere that can be drawn upon to explain the unseen spiritual side of existence. Magic is seen as the art of aligning our mind and energy fields to the greater magnetic fields and tides of the universe, and our Will with that universe so we find our true place within it.

So who, now, is Lilith? She is the dark side of woman, and that is why she has always been with us. She is the fractured half of Adam's wife, the dark destructive force that moves through the wilderness as opposed to Eve, the empty vessel's constrictive form. Like Lucifer she is the darkness that brings light, and the shadow that reflects, holding part of our soul in the daylight but invisible in the dark of which it is a part. In binding them in the darkness we have given form to our fears, in banishing them out of sight we have ensured that they are never forgotten.

There is a further darkness about Lilith that is unspoken. What made her flee, was it just *'pride'* or did Adam push her down in the dirt to lie on top of her, how hard did he insist on this right, like the animals that he had seen copulating in the field before demanding a mate? Is Lilith the first battered wife, fleeing to the wilderness rather than live in fear and loathing, then banished, reviled and replaced? Was Eve then a biblical *'Stepford wife'*, cloned off Adam to be voiceless, a part of him, a spare rib, that could only echo his will? Is this why Lilith speaks so unequivocally to feminists, out of sympathy and horror, as well as from admiration of her apparent strength and independence?

The evolution of Lilith from desert wind to embodiment of the rejected and neglected aspects of womankind is evident in all contemporary writings about her. But She has also come to symbolise the lost Goddess. Jungian writers have elucidated the realisation of this loss, and managed to convey how Lilith is one of the motherless forms of the feminine self, and the Adamah with which women need to reconnect to gain a spiritual wholeness. That Siegmund Hurwitz was one of Jung's inner circle, and a scholar of Jewish mysticism is not surprising and his book Lilith is part of the foundation literature in her contemporary study. Barbara Black Koltuv's *The Book of Lilith* is another.

Barbara Koltuv's preface encapsulates the compelling quintessence of feminine freedom and rebellion that Lilith has come to symbolise:

> "Lilith, the long haired she demon of the night, eluded this anthology for years. Eventually I began to understand. She is a force, a power, a quality, a renegade. A Free Spirit. She hates to be pinned (penned) down by the Word. It is notable that most of the words about Lilith appear in the Zohar, The Book of Splendour, a Kabbalistic work of the thirteenth century, by men,

warning other men about her powers. The weight of their words, the heavy chains of iron that bound her in the sixth century amulets intended to banish her, and the weight of Adam's body lording it over her during their marital embrace, are anathema to Lilith. They cause her to flee. And each time I attempted to write about her with words, she escaped to the edge of the Red Sea, or the wilderness, or flew up to heaven to consort with the cherubs and God, until like Solomon and Elijah, and God's three angels, I made a deal with her: I would repeat all the stories and myths and legends told by the men, and at the same time Lilith would have her Way. She anointed her body with oil and danced naked in the desert before an open fire. She danced and I watched, until I felt the meaning of her movements in my own body and soul. Only then could I begin to write of Lilith and the children of Eve" (Koltuv 1986:vii).

LILLITH, OIL ON CANVAS BY JOHN COLLIER

Lilith has become the poster girl for many Pagan women on their path of self discovery as they come to terms with their rejection of a Christian upbringing, and incorporate Pagan beliefs and practises into their own religious landscape. They reject the patriarchy, monotheism, and the male domination of an androgynous world to discover their own inner darkness. They look to the woman who was prepared to face up to the jealous destructive force of God as maker, father and judge; then take wing and fly, just like the fallen angels. They follow Lilith through her open gateway to their sense of feminine, moon-led magic, of pride in their sexuality, and to call forth their own hidden banished magical selves from the wilderness.

Working with Lilith

When I first came to magic, I knew nothing of Lilith, but the one legend of her refusing to lie under Adam and then flying out to the desert was enough, and she became the icon of my first wandering into the world of feminism. Armed with Siegmund Hurwitz, I wrote my poem to Lilith, which went on to be published, although I really knew nothing of her at all. But I was writing to myself and to my sisters, naive but raw, bringing her in from the cold, and setting us free.

When I married I came to realise that the fetters that I had railed against as a young feminist, were not fetters at all, but supports that bind the happily married man and woman. I now understand Lilith's impetuosity to be that of a young woman with the wrong partner, or worse her flight in fear from marital rape. I see the age old terror of her as due to sublimated guilt, fear of retribution of a wronged then reviled woman, fear of illicit lust that could wreak havoc in a family, and fear of death of the beloveds as punishment for lewd thoughts or deeds forbidden in primitive monotheism when procreation was all. No wonder this shadow became a demon.

Whatever Lilith was in primitive society, she is no longer, for she has become the ultimate feminist icon. She who took the name of God and flew free, immortal, independent, sexy, beautiful and strong. She who begets her demon brood with stolen seed, needing no man to rule her, queen of her domain. The worst aspects have been lost, the pain of her millennia of losses brushed over, and the danger of her demonic past wiped away like footsteps in the desert sand. She has become the symbol of free independent woman, a feminist magazine, a women's festival, she has become the free feminine itself.

Lilith is a curious depiction of the drives of Eros (love) and Thanatos (annihilation). Her reputation and exile also depict the splitting of female sexuality and gender role that has occurred in all cultures, from Lilith and Eve to the Virgin and whore of Christianity

In the end Lilith just is. Of course she has haunted all myth, all folklore, for whatever her beginnings She has become the cipher for female sexuality and feminine sexual power - that which has been inextricably linked with evil and the fall throughout the Christian era vulgaris, and further back in time. Of course then she is vampiric and dark, the seducer and the sucker of the seed, and that moment of dissolution is what men have both desired and feared to be subsumed by. She even brings the whisper of lesbian homo-eroticism in the medieval pictures of Lilith as naked serpent seducing Eve. If banished and feared of course She will emerge as seductrix in dreams.

If brought in to the light however, then what does she become? For us, now, that demon voice of the desert storm has calmed to a whisper in the wind, a whisper of an invitation, to come, to taste the apple that brings eternal life. To call her back, to welcome her from the hidden depths of our psyches as the witch arisen from the ashes of the stake, to take the throne of the Queen of Heaven. To understand that She has always been there, and it is we who yearn to fly to join her in her freedom, to deny the word of God the Father and destroyer, and to take what we want and need for our own. For it is we who yearn to dance naked by the light of her fire under the primal desert moon; then return with the dawn to our loved ones and our homes.

But, and here's the crux, we need to love Eve too, she who has been characterised as nothing but a part of Adam, the voiceless submissive second wife who brought shame and dishonour in submitting to her sister too. Her legacy is the race of mankind, brought to birth in pain; it is us, steeped in original sin, grinding the serpent of wisdom to death under our heel. This is the legacy that those who have chosen to study the Fallen reject, but they tend to reject Eve as well, when we need to forgive her, and assimilate her too if we are to find wholeness rather than create a mirror image of the split universe with all its failings.

Sylvia Brinto Perera describes the dual nature of woman, the light and dark sides of the moon which manifest in the multitude of dizygotic faces of the Goddess, in her Jungian analysis of the descent of the Goddess as a way of initiation for women. She says:

> "Psychologically, we see these two energy patterns in the empathetic and self isolating modalities that are basic to feminine psychology, in relation to all inner and outer partners – autonomous emotions and perceptions and thoughts. The active engagement that wants another, that wraps a partnership in an active loving and warring embrace – that is Inanna; the circling back and down, disinterested in the other, alone and even cold, that is Erishkigal"[46]

We need to be able to embrace both aspects, and join hands with Eve and Lilith to dance in that desert sand until in the morning they are at one. If we can heal that split, if Lilith and Eve can be recognised as sisters and reconciled, then maybe we will be able to walk a balanced line between Goddess and woman, wife and whore, lover and mother, nurturer and

---

46 Perera 1981:44

nurtured, image and reality. We could then perhaps regain the harmony of the mystic Garden of Eden, but with our eyes and hearts open. Whether this is possible remains to be seen for sexuality is part of the life force, part of the coded genetic imperative for the race to reproduce itself, and linked as sex is to our most powerful drives, and to the reproduction of the species, it will always provoke the strongest feelings, opinions, taboos and social codes.

Esoteric spirituality points us to ways in which we can throw off dogma that has been encoded in our societies for good reason, the codes that have kept the sheep on the right path on the rocky road through life. If we are prepared to face our fears, to disobey the stone cut rules of long ago, and to follow the path of enlightened free will, we may be able to walk the path between night and day, between sun and moon, between love and hate, between Thanatos and Eros. Lilith is not a fallen angel. Like many Gods she bears the imprint of human incarnation, before she transcended her ordained destiny, spoke God's secret name, and gained eternal life. She is part of us, the first woman, and thus she will always haunt the nightscapes of our dreamtime, and thus she can also show us the way through the dark, and fly with us, leaving the dirt far behind, to reach for the stars from which we are most truly formed.

Post script

This essay only reflects my current understanding of Lilith and of Fallen Angels. This has changed over the years. On putting the final key stroke to this piece the phone rang, it was Diana Allam, an Alexandrian High Priestess who has worked with Fallen Angels for decades. We chatted about this chapter, and she agreed that Lilith acts like a Fallen Angel as a teacher of the hidden ways, and suggested that as such is a child killer in that she takes away the innocence of those she touches, the innocence of the naked Adam and Eve before the fruits of the tree of knowledge made them see. She also points out that kundalini experiences often occur in women who are having sex on top, the kundalini serpent shooting up the spine in a way it cannot in missionary position. We laughed about our various mad, bad and dangerous experiences of sex, magic, aphrodisiacs and angels in our early years as experimental magicians. I had forgotten all that when I wrote this, as a woman, as a mother, as a teacher of magic. My current stance on magic is a bit of an academic feminist one, and it colours my view point as is amply demonstrated here, for those for whom Lilith is far more than I have said, for whom she remains the ultimate sexy demon of the night - long may you love her.

Selected Bibliography
MargiB – LilithGate
Http://www.bibliotecapleyades.net/sumer_anunnaki/esp_sumer_annu naki15b.htm
Hurwitz, Siegmund; *Lilith, the first Eve. Historical and Psychological Aspects of the Dark Feminine*; 1992; Daimon Verlag; Einsiedeln
Perera, Sylvia Brinton; *Descent of the Goddess, a Way of Initiation for Women*; 1981; Inner City Books; Toronto.
Scerba, Amy; *Lilith's Evolution: changing literary representations of Lilith and the evolution of a mythical heroine*; 1999; http://feminism.eserver.org/Lilith

THE FACE IN THE MIRROR

A Quest for Knowledge and Conversation with the Holy Guardian Angel

By Charlotte Rodgers

A rigid Catholic upbringing with its glamour, gilding, blood and suffering is a great foundation for a magickal practice.

Catholicism shows where ritual can take you when it works and the superficiality all the trappings and props become when faith and focus are not present.

However Catholicism was not as successful at stimulating an interest in angels in me as it had been with encouraging my interest in magick.

As a child it seemed to me that the Catholic Church had neatly delineated angels and demons into categories of name, role and whose side they are on, although they all actually seemed very similar.

Avenging angels, guardian angels, angels of light and fire and the angels that bestow pregnancy upon virgins; I was brought up with prayers addressed to them, referring to them and stained glass and sepia toned overpowering images of them.

Truth to tell I found them tedious in their golden omnipresence and perpetual role as messengers of the one true god; a god I found to be brutal, domineering and created by man in his own image.

At the age of 12 I first came across references to the fallen angels, 'The Watchers' or Grigori[47] who chose to descend to earth and procreate with human women resulting in a race of giant children the Nephilim (though there is some argument as to this interpretation of this mythology).

Now this did interest me with, partially because there was accessibility about these tales that I hadn't found in my earlier encounters with the concepts of angelic beings and also I suspect, because it appealed to some atavistic memory in me.

I think a great part of this accessibility to my then teenage self, lay in the fact that the rebellion of the 'fallen ones' reflected their making a choice and thus having an element of free will. They were not merely transmitters of messages from God.

Later in my teens I read books by Macgregor Mathers and Aleister Crowley in which reference was made to 'The Holy Guardian Angel' and whilst I devoured the literature it didn't hold quite enough glamour for me to go further than merely reading about it .

Enochian magic[48] and John Dee's work I also found fascinating but I was always put off (which is odd for me as I rarely listen to advice) by Regardie in his 'Golden Dawn' tome[49] admonishing DO NOT attempt Enochian work until you are perfected everything in this book, it is too dangerous!

Many years later the angel 'craze' hit the new age sector and whilst I found it disconcerting that the archangels that I worked with when I hit magickal black holes and needed stabilising with regular practise of the Lesser Ritual of the

---

47 In Genesis 6:1-4 the "sons of God" are captivated by the beauty of the "daughters of men." They subsequently marry them and produce an offspring of giants known as the Nephilim. Genesis goes on to say that these Nephilim were "mighty men" and "men of renown."

48 Enochian Magic is a system of ceremonial magic which invokes and commands spirits. It was based on 16th century writing of John Dee charting his work with Edward Kelly. They claimed the information which was recorded was given to them by angels.

49 Israel Regardie 'The Golden Dawn'

Pentagram[50], were being adopted (in sanitised format) and had become a spiritual version of my little pony, it didn't really have much effect on me.

When I hit my mid thirties I returned to focused magickal work.

Over the previous years I had maintained my basic spiritual interests but had primarily focused on stabilising myself and learning to live in mundane reality: thus yoga and basic earth magick and tarot work had been my main preoccupation.

Once I reaffirmed my commitment I thought it was apt to undertake some sort of focused and directional magickal working.

The Knowledge and Conversation with my Holy Guardian Angel seemed the ideal way to do this.

As I intimated earlier angels per se had originally held no particular interest for me, perhaps because I found them associative with early Christian indoctrination; but the rituals for the Knowledge and Conversation with the Holy Guardian Angel from Mathers' translation of *The Book of the Sacred Magic of Abramelin the Mage*[51] and Aleister Crowley's comments and work on the same subject that had merely intrigued me in my younger years now seemed much more relevant.

The ambiguity of the term *'Holy Guardian Angel'* lies in it being seen either as a manifestation of the true inner self or a manifestation of something beyond the self. Knowledge and conversation with either of which would eventually lead to realisation of one's true will.

---

50 Used by the Hermetic Order of the Golden Dawn this ritual which has become standard practice among many contemporary Western Mystery traditions, its primary purpose is to invoke or banish elemental forces, although this is a very simplistic way of looking at its uses
51 'The Book of the Sacred Magic of Abramelin the Mage' Translated by S.L. Macgregor Mathers

This seemed possible to tie in with other work which I have done over the years with spirit, trance, and other personal and creative magickal explorations.

It also served a secondary purpose of deconditioning prior ideas of an angel being a messenger of a Christian god and creating a concept that was valid to me rather than something non specific and homogenised for mass religious consumption and manipulation.

Although I had read more on the subject of angels at that point in my life, reading doesn't constitute a gnosis for me.

Doing and learning from experience does.

As I lived in a small flat with a housemate and necessarily needed to work for a living, taking the traditionally prescribed route over six months of rigorous life style changes was impossible; so I decided to adapt the rite.

Since my mid-teens I have used mirrors in my magickal work.

I have used them for skrying, as gateway's to other realms and as meditative and self exploratory devices.

In the latter case I would use a mirror to separate myself into subjective and objective and then explore aspects of myself related to gender, parentage, ancestry and past lives which would move through the reflections that appeared to the gazer in the mirror.

Eventually I could reach a point of knowledge of a shared universal consciousness, the oldest manifestation of self, which is beyond individual identity.

As a means of contacting spirits I would use an object or focal point that would connect me to the feel of said spirit and pull connected imagery through the gateway that my mirror had become for this purpose.

The means in which I went about the ritual to connect with my HGA were relatively simple.

I practised yoga, kept diaries and regularly used my mirror to call upon my guardian angel/guide.

Whenever I did any other ritual I would always start with a mantra to my guide although s/he was as yet unknown.

Similar in the ways in which Legba, for instance is used at the start of every voudon ritual before other god forms (or lwa in the case of voudon), are worked with.

This was a mark of respect to said Guardian Angel and in my mind part of our agreement of co operation.

I made an agreement that 'we' would create a symbiotic relationship of sorts in that my guide would give me insight and guidance as to direction and my true will, and I pacted myself to it.

Needless to say for a long time there were rituals where little seemed to happen.

Sometimes I would receive images and visuals, but not always.

The imagery I received varied its gender and was sometimes completely beyond human form.

I was able to recognise my guide from other images that appeared to me by its 'feel'.

I realised that the essence was the same but the appearance would vary.

The visuals which I saw were what I allowed myself to see or what I was capable of seeing at the time.

Although I was in contact for some time with this spirit and would receive guidance from them through divinations and glossolalia it was three years before I received the series of sounds that constituted its name, which I considered to be the cementing of our relationship.

When I finally made this full connection it came as surprise.

I had decided to perform an impromptu ritual to send love and aid for a peaceful transition to the spirits of those who had died in a terrorist attack in London.

I used a fragment of human skull (to connect with the joined human consciousness) and burnt kyphi.

As always I intoned my mantra to my Holy Guardian angel/guide and I went into a trance and had a series of images and after my asking of it, received a name.

I have wondered on occasion whether the human bone or my focusing on spirits of many who had recently died violently, acted as a catalyst for this work; or if it was simply my previous work reaching natural fruition.

Whether knowledge and conversation with my Holy Guardian Angel has changed me is a matter of perspective.

There were actions I made in my life after this contact which I felt were in accordance with my true will, that were destructive and seemingly, quite mad.

I was disorientated for quite a long time. Whether it was because of these rituals, because of various other magickal projects that I was doing at the time or just coincidence or some sort of mid life crisis I don't know.

However I realise that now, after a process of reassembling the pieces that I fractured into, I am the closest I have ever been to realising my core self.

I did learn two things.

My HGA is from outside AND from within.

I clothe this being from outside myself with what is within me.

As I smashed through the limitations of my senses, and my conditioned perceptions I was able to see/feel my HGA more fully for what it is.

My mother has maintained for many years that I have a *'something'* that looks after me, but that I had used up my allotted nine lives and should start taking more care.

Is it possible that the proverbial guardian angel is that being that puts me in such dangerous situations, and it is myself that rises beyond these dangers, which once survived leave me stripped bare from that which holds me back?

So there is my treatise on angels.

It is not a subject that is academically approached, but rather lived and experienced.

As I grow older it becomes more clear, that this is the right way for me.

HEKATE TRIFORMIS (FROM THE BOOK 'BRITISH MUSEUM', SIR HENRY ELLIS, 1836)

BETWEEN GODS AND MEN

The nature of daimons in Graeco-Roman literature, theology, and magic

By Kim Huggens

Despite the fact that the term *'demon'* is frequently used in many areas, it is little acknowledged that the term and its related concepts have their origins in the Graeco-Roman magical tradition and understanding of the human soul. And as we will see, the original concept is far more complex than our modern one, allowing room for something beyond the good/evil dichotomy.

This study of demons (which will hereafter be written daimon to reflect the Graeco-Roman conception) will explore the ancient world's view of their nature, their origin, and their relationship with both mankind and divinity. This paper will show that daimons commonly held a position in the Graeco-Roman theology between heaven and earth or earth and Hades, acting as liminal figures and mediators, as well as being the souls of the dead.

1. The Nature of Daimons – the Good, the Bad, and the Airy

It is possible to somewhat trace a development of the concept of daimons from their earliest mention in Homer to their completely reworked appearance in fourth century Christian writings, however such a survey is difficult and in places so complex that it warrants questions regarding its authenticity. As Valerie Flint writes, *"...it will never be possible to give a simple narrative account of the transmission of so essentially dynamic and emotionally charged a concept.*"[52] Instead we can examine the nature of daimons as expounded by ancient writers and briefly catch a glimpse of the development of ideas in later works.

Flint's definition of a daimon is as follows, and it is a useful starting point in our examination of the concept. It immediately removes from consideration the more modern creations of the demon:

> *"...a force, or energy, less potent than that of 'theos', or God, but far more so than that of humans. It thus came to occupy an intermediate position in the supernatural hierarchy, a position, on occasion, a little like that of a lesser god, and to be thought capable of interfering in every aspect of human endeavour, should it choose, or be compelled or invited, to do so."*[53]

Useful, but simplistic in its attempt to define a widespread concept spanning centuries. However, the dichotomy between good and evil, (between demon and angel) is immediately defunct, since it reflects the neutral nature of daimons in Graeco-Roman thought.[54]

Already fully-formed in writings of Homer, and therefore representing some of the earliest thoughts on the matter, is the idea that daimons could be both bad and good, and that the term itself was interchangeable with that of *'theos'* or god. This continues in the work of Hesiod who places daimons in a hierarchy – Gods first, daimons second, heroes third, and finally man as lowest. Further, daimons formed two classes, that of the

---

52 Flint, Witchcraft and Magic in Europe, Vol. 2: Ancient Greece and Rome, pp. 290.
53 Flint, Witchcraft and Magic in Europe, Vol. 2: Ancient Greece and Rome, pp. 281
54 Another useful examination of the term "daimon" in Greek thought and particularly in Homer can be found in Samuel E. Bassett's "Δαιμων in Homer", in The Classical Review, vol. 33, no. 7/8 (Nov-Dec, 1919), pp. 134-136. In it he writes, "The word δαιμων has been generally understood to mean in the Homeric poems either a god or, more commonly, indefinite and not clearly personalised divine power; in the latter sense its use seems to have been not unlike that of our word 'Heaven' as distinguished from 'God'."

'higher' or benevolent daimons, and that of the 'lower' or bad daimons.[55] Both classes of daimons, Hesiod says, were worshiped by the Greeks – a practice he seems to condemn, eager to point out that people should not mistake the daimons for the spirits of dead heroes.[56] Later writers also held a similar hierarchy for daimons, and added that daimons could, very rarely, become Gods through their good acts – a notable example is that given by Plutarch of Isis and Osiris, who were originally daimons who were deified by the Gods.[57] In later writings it is stated that after death men could become benevolent daimons, but wicked men could become malevolent daimons, wandering the earth aimlessly and harming mortals.

There are many examples of daimons behaving badly (falling into Hesiod's 'lower' class of daimons) in early Greek literature, terrorizing and harming humans or deceiving them. Pausanias writes of a story he heard, in which the city of Temesa stoned to death a man who raped a young woman. The daimon (spirit) of this man (later identified as Lycas or 'wolf-man') returned to haunt the city, killing people at will. Obviously upset, the citizens asked their oracle for advice, and were told to instate a yearly gift of a young woman as the daimon's 'bride' (human sacrifice). They did so for many years, until a hero (Euthymus) came upon their yearly ritual, and requested to see the woman chosen as the bride. Seeing her he fell in love, and when night fell he waited for the daimon of Lycas, attacked him, and drove him into the sea from which he never returned. [58] This story not only highlights the fact that daimons were also

---

55 Hesiod, Works and Days, vv.109-93
56 For further comments on Hesiod's view of hero-worship, see Luck, Arcana Mundi, pp. 228-9.
57 Plutarch, On Isis and Osiris 26-27, pp.361 A-E. He mentions in this text that Heracles and Dionysus received similar promotion from the ranks of benevolent daimons to that of Gods, and like Isis and Osiris they received worship as both daimons and Gods – fittingly so, because their powers were especially concerning what is "above the earth" as well as "below the earth".
58 Pausanias, Description of Greece 6.6. Compare this story to the above passage from Apuleius, De Deo Socratis, wherein lesser souls become malevolent daimons after death.

thought to be the spirits of the dead (more correctly called *nekydaimones*) but also that daimons were often worshiped or given offerings (more on this later.)

2. The Demon on my Shoulder

Not only could daimons be good or bad, but they had a direct relationship with human beings. Pindar writes that benevolent daimons could bring luck, riches, and a long happy life to people and should therefore be worked with and given rewards,[59] whilst malevolent daimons could bring illness and death, and should be opposed.[60] He also writes that every human on earth is given a *'guardian spirit'* daimon,[61] and Apuleius holds the same idea.[62] Although everybody has their own *'guardian daimon'*, not everybody had the power to meet it, but magic could be used to contact it. Porphyry reports a magical operation performed for Plotinus to meet his guardian daimon, in which it was discovered Plotinus had no ordinary spirit for a familiar but instead a God! [63] Plato himself believed in this guardian daimon, and stated that:

> "...God has given to each of us as his daemon, that kind of soul which is housed in the top of our body and which raises us – seeing that we are not an earthly but a heavenly plant – up from the earth towards our kindred in heaven."[64]

However, some writers did not just believe in a guardian daimon, but also in an accompanying malevolent daimon. This daimon presumably served to counteract the good daimon, drawing the individual's mind back to the earth; however it may also have been the writer's aim to find a cosmic or theological excuse for mankind's immoral decisions and wrongdoings.[65]

---

59 Pindar, Olympian 9.110, and Pythian 103-111 and 10.10.
60 Isthmian Odes 7.40-45 and Nemean 9.27.
61 Pindar, Pythian 5.164ff
62 Apuleius, De Deo Socratis 15-16
63 Porphyry, Life of Plotinus 10, 56-60.
64 Plato, Timaeus 90CC.
65 Plutarch, Brutus 36.3-4.

3. Between Heaven and Earth

It was also common in the Greek and Latin literature to view daimons as intermediaries between man and the Gods – possibly inspired by Hesiod's hierarchy. Plutarch writes that daimons are the servants of Gods in the earthly realm, and that the Gods prefer not to get involved directly but instead act through daimons! (Indeed, it seems Plutarch is aware of Hesiod's hierarchy, since he mentions the distinction between good and bad daimons.) He writes:

> *But there are those who have discovered that the race of daemons, halfway between gods and men, communicates between the gods and mankind and establishes a relationship between them and us...*"[66]

Plato is undoubtedly the inspiration behind Plutarch's writing since he is mentioned as one of the foremost expounders of the theory. Plato also held that daimons, due to their intermediary role between gods and men, were placed in charge of all oracles, divinations, and ensured that sacrifices and offerings made their way to the gods:

> *"...interpreting and transporting human beings to the gods and divine things to men; entreaties and sacrifices from below, and ordinances and requitals from above: being midway between, it makes each to supplement the other, so that the whole is combined in one. Through [the daimon] are conveyed all divination and priestcraft concerning sacrifice and ritual and incantations, and all soothsaying and sorcery. God with man does not mingle: but the spiritual is the means of all society and converse of men with gods and of gods with men..."*[67]

Iamblichus, also clearly inspired by Plato's work, identifies daimons as spirits of the air, changing divine energies into forms that mankind can understand and put to use.[68] Further, the fact that they inhabit a realm between heaven and earth causes some daimons to become contaminated by the earthly passions

---

66 Plutarch, On the Ceasing of Oracles 9-11, pp. 414E-415A.
67 Plato, Timaeus, 3.178-9.
68 Iamblichus, On the Mysteries 1.5

that humans engage in, rather than the lofty ideals of the divine. Such daimons become malevolent, and later go on to harm humans.[69] In this case, it is the earth and the human realm that is lowly, rather than the realm the daimon inhabits, as is common in later medieval theology. Iamblichus is one of the writers who most clearly distinguished between Gods and daimons, further enabling the view of them as mediators between Gods and humans.[70] He makes this distinction based on the visibility or invisibility of daimons and the power that Gods wield over them.[71] He also differentiates (quite atypically of Late Antique period) between daimons, heroes, and souls, once again based on their powers. The power of daimons:

> "...is productive: it fashions the cosmic organisms and completes the perfection of every single living creature [...] To the daemons one must attribute the generative powers that control the organism and the connection of the soul and body."[72]

The idea of daimons as mediators between heaven and earth is continued into Jewish Hellenistic theology by Philo Judaeus of Alexandria, who was writing in the first century CE and one of the scholars of the intellectual melting pot of Alexandria (therefore his ideas were highly likely to have had a great influence upon any later work, in particular early Christian theology.) In Philo's work daimons were the airy ambassadors of God, building bridges between man and God. Even the malevolent daimons were under God's control, and were used by God as a means of punishing human wrongdoing.[73]

---

69 Ibid, 1.10-15, 18-20, and 2.6.
70 This detailed distinction and description of the nature of daimons and Gods is so important to Iamblichus because, as George Luck writes, "It was important to recognize the true character of a vision. It could be dangerous, or at least embarrassing, to mistake a god for a mere guardian spirit, or vice versa. Hence the subject also had a practical value." (Arcana Mundi, pp. 275.)
71 Iamblichus, On the Mysteries, 1.20.61-63
72 Ibid, 2.1.67-2.69
73 Philo of Alexandria, On the Giants, 3-4.

However by the time of the early church fathers and the writings of Eusebius[74] and Augustine, conceptions of daimons had become far more negative. Instead of being ambassadors of God similar to angels, daimons had become tricksters and deceivers, and any individuals worshipping them were worshipping a base spirit lower even than man. Somehow, the daimon's higher place in the cosmology of the universe had been lost and they had been relegated to something lower than human. Augustine writes:

> "We can by no means accept the theory which Apuleius does his best to prove... namely, that demons are situated midway between gods and men and serve as intermediaries and interpreters, that is to carry our petitions from earth, and to bring back help from the gods. On the contrary we should believe that they are spirits fanatically bent on doing harm, completely at odds with justice, swollen with pride, green with envy and well practised in deceit, who live, it is true, in our air, but do so because they were cast out from the lofty regions of the higher heavens..."[75]

There is little to suggest how such a dramatic change could take place in the view of daimons in the space of a few centuries.[76] However, it seems that Augustine may have been familiar with some of the more unsavoury magical practises associated with the use of malevolent daimons by Greek magicians (further explored later), as he identifies his conception of daimons as being employed in Greek magic.[77] However, in this writing the magician is painted as the tool used by the daimon rather than the earlier Greek form wherein the magician is in control of the employed daimon.

---

74 Eusebius, The Preparation of the Gospel, 4.5.1-3
75 Augustine, City of God, 8.22.
76 Valerie Flint suggests that the transference of the concept of demons vs. angels in Christianity came from the debate between Iamblichus and Porphyry regarding good/evil daimons and their use in theurgy and magic. See Witchcraft and Magic in Europe, Vol. 2: Ancient Greece and Rome, pp. 284-289.
77 Augustine, City of God, 8.18-19.

4. "Search the Regions of the Dead, Send this Daimon..."

Such magic[78] performed with daimons employed a specific kind of daimon: the nekydaimon, or spirit of the dead. As we have already seen, on a few occasions the ancient writers distinguish between the souls of humans and daimons, however it is a far more common feature of these periods to view daimons as the part of man that we might call his ghost, spirit,[79] or shade.[80] More specifically, it is the part of man's soul that often becomes trapped between the worlds – between the living earth of humankind and the afterlife of Hades or Elysium.[81]

As early as Homer we find this idea already fully formed, and we are furnished with a narration of Odysseus' attempt to summon daimons from Hades in order to gain information (a common practice, and as we have seen above is akin to the oracles caused by daimons). In the *Odyssey* the eponymous hero desires information from the dead seer Tiresias, and to get it he digs a ditch and pours libations of honey, milk, wine, and blood. This ditch acts as a liminal point between Hades and earth, so Odysseus is both above the earth and below it, and allows the dead to escape.[82] Interestingly, in this account the dead rise from Hades in the order in which they descended, so Odysseus meets a great many daimons before he reaches

---

78 PGM IV. 448.

79 Indeed, in Plutarch's Consolation Addressed to Apollonius 14, a man raises up the daimon of his dead son, which speaks to him directly, saying "I am the soul of your son". This has been interpreted to indicate a daimon, and it certainly displays all the same characteristics as daimons from Homer and Hesiod, but the word used for 'soul' in this instance is ψυχαι, a term more adequately describing a soul or spirit.

80 Such distinctions and hierarchies for daimons provoked one writer to ask the question, Do daimons die? Plutarch wrote a dialogue between Cleombrotus and Heracleon in which he supposed that by saying they were immortal they were no different to Gods, which would be absurd, but saying they die like men would also be so. Instead, he tells a story of the report of the death of a daimon who had presided over an oracle. (On the Ceasing of Oracles 14-15, pp. 418E-419E.)

81 For an excellent study of the relationship between the living and the dead in ancient Greece, see Sarah Iles Johnston, Restless Dead: Encounters Between the Living and the Dead in Ancient Greece.

82 Homer, Odyssey, 11.12-224.

Tiresias, including the daimon of his own mother.[83] It is also interesting that the daimons clamour to drink from the blood – it was believed that by drinking the blood of animals or humans they could regain some semblance of life – similar, in a way, to vampires.[84] Offerings to daimons suggest further that the distinction between them and Gods was blurred: they were spirits just as the Gods were, but certainly lesser in power.

Such nekydaimones played such a large role in Graeco-Roman magic that they are not only recorded in the original texts of the magical operations themselves, but also parodied and narrated by the Greek and Latin dramatists and novelists. Examining their use in the magical texts, we find a lot of material that reveals more about their nature.

We know that daimons were commonly raised from Hades by a magician or witch in order to gain information (necromancy)[85], to search for the victim of the spell and 'fetch' him/her for the operator, to enact the results of a malefic or erotic spell, or to torment or bring illness and death to the victim of the spell. They may also possess the living and bring about illnesses, bad fortune, and social ineptitude! Philostratus writes of a young man who is what our modern sensibilities would label as 'camp', brash, and rude, but who becomes a modest gentleman upon exorcism.[86]

Many magical texts inform us how daimons were raised by magicians for their purposes. For instance, one particularly gruesome erotic spell from the Graeco-Roman Magical Papyri

---

83 For an interesting article on the quality of information given by the daimon of Odysseus' mother, see Frederik M. Combellack, "Odysseus and Anticleia", in Classical Philology, vol. 69, no. 2, (Apr., 1974), pp. 121-123.

84 Note the relation to the human sacrifice given to the daimon Lycas in Pausanias' Description of Greece, discussed above.

85 For example, PGM IV. 1323-30, and the previously discussed magical rite performed by Odysseus.

86 See Philostratus, Life of Apollonius of Tyana, 4.20. Possession is also implied in PGM IV. 1227-64, "Excellent rite for driving out daimons". This magical text doesn't detail the symptoms of possession as Philostratus does, but does give a method for removing the daimon!

(PGM) demonstrates how infernal gods and daimons are called upon to assist the specific daimon identified by the magician for the enactment of the spell's effects (in this case the tormenting of the desired victim).[87] In PGM IV.2714-83 the daimons are described as belonging to the chthonic goddess Hekate, and as breathing fire, hissing wildly and holding anger in their hearts. The concept that daimons must be raised through appeal to their masters and mistresses is common throughout the PGM: Hekate and other chthonic gods such as Hades, Persephone, and Erishkigal are often called upon first and beseeched to release daimons suitable to the task. See, for instance, PGM IV. 1390-1495, in which the magician goes to a place where heroes or gladiators have died by violence, and invokes various Underworld deities to *"Send up to me the phantoms of the dead forthwith for service in this very hour."* (1468-9). This is very similar to the prayer to Helios (though not a chthonic god he appears to have either been worshipped by the particular magician who owned this magical handbook, or to have been given power over all the world) in PGM IV. 445-447:

> *"And even now I beg you, blessed one, / Unfailing one, the master of the world, / If you go to the depths of the earth and search the regions of the dead, send this daimon, / From whose body I hold this remnant in my hands..."*

It is also a formula repeated in PGM III. 230: *"Send me the daimon who will give responses to me about everything which I order him to speak about"*

From such texts we can glean an idea of where it is that daimons were believed to preside. The general consensus appears to be that they inhabit the realms of the Underworld (from which they cannot escape unless the chthonic gods release them), but that they also have a physical connection to their place of burial.[88] Thus, magicians are frequently advised to

---

87 PGM IV, 296-466, "Wondrous Spell for Binding a Lover".
88 See Plato, Phaedrus, 81c-d.

go to the graves of those untimely dead, the burial places of gladiators and heroes, or any cemetery, to perform their rites.[89] It is usually specified that the burial place chosen must be that of somebody who has died before their time, or unmarried, without children, or dead by violence.[90] Tertullian enlightens us as to the reason for this: such daimons were bitter because their time had been cut short, and therefore more likely to aid the magician in his nefarious ends.[91] It is also suggested by Virgil that the untimely dead are barred entry to Hades proper and thus reside in the limbo of the banks of the river Styx, the ferryman refusing to row them across. Thus, they may prove easier to raise than the happily dead.[92]

The daimon in the ancient world was often believed to have a connection not just to its burial place but also to its corpse. Daniel Ogden has examined the practices of *"ghost hobbling"*, in which a body part from the corpse of a daimon expected to become harmful towards the living would be mutilated or twisted/turned around in some way.[93] This may have originally risen from a sympathetic understanding of the relation between spirit and corpse, and thus the spirit is afflicted with an inability to act or to move just as the corpse is symbolically prevented from doing so. In magical texts we find that the magician often held a piece of the daimon's corpse hostage so that it would do as requested of it: in a papyrus that was found accompanying an effigy in 3rd century Egypt the daimon Antinous is told that

---

89 Such as in PGM III. 1-164, where a cat is sacrificed and laid in a tomb or grave, and the rest of the raising of the daimon takes place there. Also PGM IV. 299-466, where an effigy of the victim is placed in the "grave of one untimely dead", and the daimon of that grave is then called upon to lead a search party of daimons to fetch the victim for the magician and bring her torments.

90 Ogden highlights, with reference to Homer, several different categories defined by different Greek terms for the many types of restless dead, including αοροι – those dead before their time; αγαμοι – those dead before marriage; βιαιοθανατοι – those dead by violence. See Magic, Witchcraft and Ghosts in the Greek and Roman Worlds: A Source Book, pp. 146.

91 Tertullian in De Anima 56-7.

92 Virgil, Aeneid, 6.325-30; 426-443.

93 See Ogden, Magic, Witchcraft and Ghosts in the Greek and Roman Worlds: A Source Book, pp. 162.

he will not be released and his body part not returned to his grave until he has fulfilled the magician's wishes.[94] From the same period but in Athens a figurine used for a curse was discovered in a grave in which the corpse had been mutilated and had several body parts removed.[95] It may be out of fear of this control over daimons using their corpses that many graves were guarded with curses to prevent break-ins.[96] Further, there appears to have been a widespread fear of the daimon attacking the magician that disturbs its grave for such purposes.[97] In the humorous epic *The Golden Asse by Apuleius*, we are given a bawdy tale of a man who agrees to guard a corpse overnight and protect it against Thessalian witches eager to bite pieces of the corpses face off for use in their spells – something the mourning family were extremely frightened of.[98]

However, it was possible for the magician to create a daimon suited for his purpose, thus removing the need to dig up corpses and wander around graveyards. In PGM III.1-164 the cat that is sacrificed has its daimon roused to serve the magician alongside the daimons of the cemetery;[99] Virgil's Dido added her own body to the magical fire, and sent her own daimon after her victim[100]; Lucan's Erictho (a marvellous parody of a witch, but one certainly set in fact as shown by the texts from the PGM!) is repeatedly described as committing murders and killing unborn children ripped from their mother's wombs to serve her magically.[101]

---

94 R. Daniel and F. Maltomini, Supplementum Magicum, 47.

95 D.R. Jordan, "New Archaeological Evidence for the Practice of Magic in Classical Athens" in Praktika of the 12th International Congress of Classical Archaeology, 273-77.

96 An excellent article on this subject can be found by J.H.M. Strubbe, "Cursed be he that moves my bones" in C. Faraone and D. Obbink eds. Magika Hiera: Ancient Greek magic and religion, pp. 33-59.

97 See Daniel Ogden, Witchcraft and Magic in Europe, vol .2: Ancient Greece and Rome, pp. 17-18.

98 Apuleius, The Golden Asse or Metamorphoses, 2.21-30.

99 It is also interesting that in this text, the term αγγελος (angel, or messenger) is used to address the cat's daimon.

100 Virgil, Aeneid 4.641-65

101 Lucan, Pharsalia, 6.413-830.

5. Conclusion

In these magical operations involving daimons we see a marked difference in the nature of these daimons to those of Plato or Plutarch. It is conceivable that these nekydaimones form Hesiod's 'lower' class of daimons, but certainly they are closer in nature to the later medieval variants. However, the philosophers and theologians of the ancient world have as their daimons mediators, spiritual bridge-builders, guardian spirits, and entities that are undeniably neutral and – perhaps most importantly – useful to both Gods and men, and which form an indispensable part of the make-up of and continuation of the universe itself.

Source Texts

Apuleius; *De Deo Socratis*; Online at http://www.thelatinlibrary.com/apuleius.html

Bettenson, Henry (trans); *Augustine, The City of God*; 2003; Oxford World Classics; Oxford

Betz, Hans Deiter (trans); *The Greek Magical Papyri in Translation, Vol 1: Texts*; 1996; University of Chicago Press; Chicago

Daniel, R.W., & Maltomini, F. (eds); *Supplementum Magicum. Papyrologica Coloniensia*. Vols. 16.1 and 16.2. 2 vols; 1990–92

Gifford, Edwin (trans); *Eusebius, Preparation for the Gospel*; 2002; Wipf & Stock Publishers

Goodwin, William W.; *Plutarch, On the Cessation of Oracles. In Plutarch's Morals*; 1878; Little, Brown, and Co.

Jones, Peter, & Rieu, E.V. (trans); *Homer, Odyssey*; 2003; Oxford World Classics; Oxford

Jones, W.H.S., & Ormerod, H.A. (trans); *Pausanias, Description of Greece* Bks.VI-VIII, xxi v. 3; 1977; Loeb Classical Library

Joyce, Jane Wilson (trans); *Lucan, Pharsalia*; 1993; Cornell University Press; New York

Lee, Desmond (trans); *Plato, Timaeus and Critias*; 2008; Penguin Classics; London

Mackenna, Stephen (trans); *Porphyry, The Essence of Plotinus: Extracts from the Six Enneads and Porphyry's Life of Plotinus*; 1998; Kessinger Publishing

Mead, G.R.S. (trans); *Plutarch, Concerning the Mysteries of Isis and Osiris*; 2005; Kessinger Publishing

Perrin, Bernadette (trans); *Plutarch, Lives: Dion and Brutus, Timoleon and Aemilius Paulus*; 1918; Loeb Classical Library

Philostratus; *Life of Apollonius of Tyana*, Vol.1, Bks. 1-4; 2005; Loeb Classical Library

Roberts, Reverend Alexander (ed); *Tertullian, De Anima* in *The Ante-Nicene Fathers: The Writings of the Fathers Down to A.D. 325*, Vol. III *Latin Christianity: Its Founder, Tertullian -Three Parts: 1. Apologetic; 2. Anti-Marcion*; 3. Ethical; 2007; Cosimo Inc

Taylor, Thomas (trans); *Iamblichus, On the Mysteries of the Egyptians, Chaldeans and Assyrians*; 2006; Cruzian Mystic Books

Verity, Anthony (trans); *Pindar, The Complete Odes*; 2007; Oxford World Classics; Oxford

Walsh, P.G. (trans); *Apuleius, The Golden Asse*; 1999; Oxford World Classics; Oxford

Waterfield, Robin (trans); *Plato, Phaedrus*; 2002; Oxford World Classics; Oxford

West, David (trans); *Virgil, Aeneid*; 2003; Penguin Calssics; London

West, M.L. (trans); *Hesiod, Theogony and Works and Days*; 1999; Oxford Paperbacks; Oxford

Yonge, Charles Duke (trans); *The Works of Philo Judaeus, the contemporary of Josephus*; 1854-1890; H.G. Bohn

Secondary Texts
Bassett, Samuel E.; Δαιμων *in Homer*; 1919; in *The Classical Review*, 33.7/8:134-136

Combellack, Frederik M., *Odysseus and Anticleia*; 1974; in *Classical Philology* 69.2:121-123.

Dickie, Matthew W.; *Magic and Magicians in the Greco-Roman World*; 2002; Routledge; London

Faraone, C., & Obbink, D. (eds); *Magika Hiera: Ancient Greek Magic and Religion*; 1991; Oxford University Press; Oxford

Flint et. al.; *Witchcraft and Magic in Europe, Vol 2: Ancient Greece and Rome*; 1999; Athlone Press; London

Graf, Fritz; *Magic in the Ancient World*; 1999; Harvard University Press; Harvard

Luck, George; *Arcana Mundi: Magic and the Occult in the Greek and Roman Worlds*; 2006; John Hopkins University Press; Maryland

Johnston, Sarah Iles; *Restless Dead: Encounters Between the Living and the Dead in Ancient Greece*; 1999; University of California Press; California

Jordan, D.R.; *New Archaeological Evidence for the Practice of Magic in Classical Athens*; 1983; in *Praktika of the 12th International Congress of Classical Archaeology*, 273-77.

Ogden, Daniel; *Greek and Roman Necromancy*; 2004; Princeton University Press; Princeton

-----------; *Magic, Witchcraft and Ghosts in the Greek and Roman Worlds: A Source Book*; 2002; Oxford University Press; Oxford

ZOROASTRIAN
ANGELS AND DEMONS

By Payam Nabarz

> *"I confess myself a worshipper of Mazda(Wise), a follower of Zarathushtra, one who hates the Daevas(demons), and obeys the laws of Ahura (Lord); For sacrifice, prayer, propitiation, and glorification unto [Havani], the holy and master of holiness. . . Unto Mithra, the lord of wide pastures, who has a thousand ears, ten thousand eyes..."*

Zoroastrian Hymn to Mithra[102]

One of the oldest examples of the gods of one religion becoming the demons of another is perhaps seen in late Hinduism and late Zoroastrianism. This disparity can be viewed as a wave of new gods and their people battling the older gods and their worshippers. The Zoroastrian God and Angels are called Ahuras (Lords) and Zoroastrian false gods or demons are called Dev (Daevas), while in Hinduism the Gods are called Deva and demons Asuras (Ahuras). The positioning of Ahuras versus Devas is a later development in both religions, while in earlier periods they were seen as gods worshiped by different people: those of Indo-Iranian/ Indo-European (Aryans) origins and the followers of the native Vedic religions of India.[103] The spread of the Aryan pantheon into India and the subsequent blending of

---

102 'Hymn to Mithra', from the Avesta in Sacred Books of the East, Darmester (trans), 1898.
103 A History of Religious Ideas, M. Eliade.

Aryan gods and Vedic gods provides the rich and diverse pantheon present in India today. In addition to Hinduism the Deva are seen in a more positive light than the Asuras in Buddhism too. However, the focus and scope of this article is the Zoroastrian form of Ahuras and Devas, rather than the Hindu or Buddhist interpretations.

The Prophet Zarathustra (the Greek name of Zoroaster) was a religious reformer, priest, visionary and prophet who brought about what could be seen as the reformation of Persian polytheism. The end product was probably the world's first monotheistic religion, long before Judaism, Christianity and Islam. There are differing views regarding whether Zoroaster even predates the Pharaoh Akhenaten and his monotheistic worship of the Aten. Zoroaster formed a new religion out of the old Persian forms of worship and different tribal religions and regional sects. Over many more centuries, this religion, Zoroastrianism, slowly gained in popularity and finally became the state religion of the Persian Empire until the rise of Islam. This religion continued to be practised despite pressure and persecution by some Islamic rulers; it is still being practised today, with followers across the globe.

Zoroaster is thought to have lived in north eastern Iran sometime in the sixth or fifth century BCE, though some scholars believe it could have been as early as 1400 BCE. Zoroaster is said to have had a miraculous birth: his mother, Dughdova, was a virgin who conceived him after being visited by a shaft of light. Zoroaster's teachings led to the world's first monotheistic religion, in which Ahura Mazda, the *'Wise Lord'* of the sky, was the ultimate creator. In this religious reform, many gods and goddesses of the Persian pantheon were stripped of their sovereignty and their powers and attributes were bestowed upon the one god; Ahura Mazda.

The *Avesta* is the Zoroastrian holy book. It is a collection of holy texts, which include the *Gathas* (the word of the prophet

Zoroaster himself) and the *Yashts*, the ancient liturgical poems and hymns that scholars believe predated Zoroaster and were modified to reflect the reformation. It also contains rituals, precepts for daily life and rites of passage for birth, marriage, and death. Because of the *Avesta*, the Zoroastrians were the first *'people of the book'*. Avesta probably means *'authoritative utterance.'*[104]

The *Gathas* are seen as the original teaching by the Prophet Zoroaster. Other texts in the *Avesta* belong to the Zoroastrian body of texts, some of which predate Zoroaster and some are later than Zoroaster himself. In some cases, like that of Zurvanism, it is referred to as an offshoot and a heresy. The scope of this article is the whole of the *Avesta* and the Zoroastrian body of texts and not limited to the *Gathas*. In the *Gathas* the concept of angels and demons are abstract figures and ideas, while in earlier texts and later texts they are substantive figures and beings.

Some of the *Yashts* are hymns to ancient Persian deities, who in Zoroastrianism are demoted to the ranks of archangels or angels, with Ahura Mazda at the top of the hierarchy. In the Zoroastrian religion, Ahura Mazda has seven immortal aspects - the Amshaspends or Spenta Mainyu (Ameshas Spenta), each of which rules over a particular realm. These holy heptads are: Vohu Mano (good thought, the realm of animals), Asha Vahishta (righteousness, the realm of fire), Spenta Armaiti (devotion, the realm of earth), Khshathra Vairya (dominion, the realm of air, sun and heavens), Haurvatat (wholeness, the realm of water), Ameretat (immortality, the realm of plants), and Spenta Mainyu, who is identified with Ahura Mazda (the realm of humanity). There are also seven Yazatas, the protective spirits: Anahita (water / fertility), Atar (fire), Homa (the healing plant), Sraosha (obedience / hearer of prayers), Rashnu (judgment), Mithra

---

104 Zoroastrianism, P. Clark

(truth), Tishtrya (the Dog Star / source of rain).[105] These can be seen in the following diagram.

Zoroastrianism is monotheistic, with a strong sense of dualism, whereby Ahura Mazda's Ameshas Spenta and Yazatas, the forces of light and Truth (*Asha*), are faced with the forces of darkness of the Angra Mainyu, or Ahriman, who is called the Great Lie (*Druj*). He and his demons are said to create drought, harsh weather, sickness, disease, poverty, and all forms of suffering. The holy heptads the Amshaspends are faced by the unholy heptads, their polar opposites and antithesis.

Arch demons	*Archangels*
Angra Mainyu (main)	*Spenta Mainyu (main)*
Indra	*Asha Vahishta*
Sauru	*Khshathra Vairya*
Naunghaithya	*Spenta Armaiti*
Tauru	*Haurvatat*
Zairi	*Ameretat*
Akem Mano	*Vohu-mano*

There were sixteen perfect lands/countries created by Ahura Mazda and as many plagues created by Angra Mainyu to destroy them. Here are some of examples:

---

105 The Ultimate Encyclopaedia of Mythology, Cotterell

Plagues sent by Angra Mainyu	Main characteristic of the land or peoples created Ahura Mazda
Snakes	Rivers
Locusts	Pastures for the plants
Plundering by soldiers and thieves	Strength to the people and land allowing defence to be achieved
Ants	Corn fields
Doubt	Faith
Created tears and wailing	Mourning by leaving the house
Idolatry	Belief
The Sin of Pride	Rich pastures
Unnatural sin	(Not clear)
Burying the dead	Beauty of the landscape

Angra Mainyu creates 99,999 diseases; Ahura Mazda counters with the Holy Mantra and with the Airyaman prayer.

The Greek writer Plutarch also refers to the holy heptads:

"XLVII. They too, nevertheless, tell many fabulous stories concerning their gods—for example, the following: that Oromazes (Ahura Mazda) sprang out of the purest Light, but Arimanios (Ahriman/ Angra Mainyu) out of Darkness; they wage war upon each other. Oromazes created six gods, the first of Goodwill, the second of Truth, the third of Order, of the rest one of Wisdom, one of Wealth, one of Pleasure in things beautiful. The other God created, as it were, opponents to these deities, equal in number. Then Oromazes, having augmented himself threefold, severed from the Sun as much space as the Sun is distant from Earth, and adorned the heavens with stars; and one star he appointed before all for guard and look out, namely Sirius. And having created four-and-twenty other gods, he shut them up in an egg; but those made by Arimanios, being as many as they, pierced the egg that had been laid, and so the bad things were mixed up with the good. But a time appointed by fate is coming, *in which Arimanios having brought on famine and pestilence must needs be destroyed by the same and utterly vanish; when the earth becoming plain and level there shall be one life and one government of men, all happy and of one language"*[106]

The battle wages across all realms, in the Zoroastrian *Vendidad* texts the Daevas are named:

"10.9 I drive away Indra, I drive away Sauru, I drive away the daeva Naunghaithya, from this house, from this borough, from this town, from this land; from the very body of the man defiled by the dead, from the very body of the woman defiled by the dead; from the master of the house, from the lord of the borough, from the lord of the town, from the lord of the land; from the whole of the world of Righteousness. I drive away Tauru, I drive away Zairi, from this house, from this borough, from this town, from this land; from the very body of the man defiled by the dead, from the very body of the woman defiled by the dead; from the master of the house, from the lord of the borough, from the lord of the town, from the lord of the land; from the whole of the holy world."[107]

And furthermore:

"19.43. They cried about, their minds wavered to and fro, Angra Mainyu the deadly, the Daeva of the Daevas; Indra the Daeva, Sauru the Daeva, Naunghaithya the Daeva, Taurvi and Zairi; Aeshma of the murderous spear; Akatasha the Daeva; Winter, made by the Daevas; the deceiving, unseen Death; Zaurva, baneful to the fathers; Buiti the Daeva; Driwi the Daeva; Daiwi the Daeva; Kasvi the Daeva; Paitisha the most Daeva-like amongst the Daevas. And the evil-doing Daeva, Angra Mainyu, the deadly, said: What! let the wicked, evil-doing Daevas gather together at the head of Arezura (gate of hell)! They rush away shouting, the wicked, evil-doing Daevas; they run away shouting, the wicked, evil doing Daevas; they run away casting the Evil Eye, the wicked, evil-doing Daevas: Let us gather together at the head of Arezura! For he is just born the holy Zarathushtra, in the house of Pourushaspa. How can we procure his death? He

---

106 Plutarch's Morals, King
107 Vendidad, Sacred Books of the East, Darmesteter (Peterson)

is the weapon that fells the fiends: he is a counter-fiend to the fiends; he is a Druj to the Druj. Vanished are the Daeva worshippers, the Nasu made by the Daeva, the false-speaking Lie! They rush away shouting, the wicked, evil-doing Daevas, into the depths of the dark, raging world of hell."[108]

Other examples of binary opposites in creation are: when Ahura Mazda created the stars and constellations, Ahriman created the planets; when Ahura Mazda created the dog, Ahriman created the wolf; when Ahura Mazda created cattle and domestic animals Ahriman created animals of their opposite. Plutarch mentions a rite to Ahriman where some of his animals are listed:

> *"XLVI. And this is the opinion of most men, and those the wisest, for they believe, some that there are Two Gods, as it were of opposite trades—one the creator of good, the other of bad things; others call the better one "God," the other "Dæmon," as did Zoroaster the Magian, who, they record, lived 5,000 years before the Trojan War. He therefore calls the former "Oromazes," the latter "Arimanios;" and furthermore explains that of all the objects of sense, the one most resembles Light, the other Darkness, and Ignorance; and that Mithras is between the two, for which reason the Persians call Mithras the "Mediator," and he [Zoroaster] taught them to offer sacrifice of vows and thanksgiving to the one, of deprecation and mourning to the other. For they bruise a certain herb called "omoine" in a mortar and invoke Hades sand Darkness, and mixing it with the blood of a wolf they have sacrificed, they carry away and throw it into a place where the Sun never comes, for of plants they believe some to belong to the good God, others to the evil Dæmon; and similarly of animals, dogs, birds, and land hedgehogs belong to the Good, but to the Bad One water rats, for which reason they hold happy men that have killed the greatest number of such things."[109]*

---

108 Vendidad, Sacred Books of the East, Darmesteter (Peterson)
109 Plutarch's Morals, King

The Zoroastrian dualistic idea of Good versus Evil was inherited by Judaism and then Christianity and Islam; indeed, it is possible to trace the axis of evil-versus-good theology and mentality from Zoroaster to all the current monotheistic world religions. The Zoroastrian scholar Mary Boyce describes the Zoroastrian text about *Viraz's* vision of heaven and hell as the ultimate source of Dante's *Divine Comedy*.

- The Zoroastrian sequence of legends of *'saviour'* and *'anti -saviour'* figures has many parallels with the *Book of Revelations*. To illustrate some of parallels:
- The theme of the saviour (Saoshyant) sent from god.
- The antichrist (evil sent from Ahriman).
- The whore of Babylon (Jeh the whore).
- The last judgment (*Frashegrid*).
- The end of times (*Khshathra*), and the resurrection of the dead.
- The fiery horseman to bring the world to end.

In this Zoroastrian eternal battle of light and darkness, Mithra is the great warrior who, according to his hymn (*Yasht 10*), carries the hundred-knotted mace or club with a hundred edges, *"the strongest of all weapons, the most victorious of all weapons, from whom Angra Mainyu, who is all death, flees away with fear."* (Today, Zoroastrian priests still carry the mace of Mithra, which is given to them at their ordination as a symbol of fighting evil.) Even though the old gods were stripped of their power, Mithra had such wide popularity and importance that the Zoroastrians adapted the stories concerning him and gave him a prominent place in their religion.

The end times is referred to by Plutarch:

> *"Theopomus (born c. 380 B.C.) says that, according to the Magians, for three thousand years alternatively the one god will dominate the other and be dominated, and that for another three thousand years they will fight and*

make war, until one smashes up the domain of the other. In the end Hades (Ahriman) shall perish and men shall be happy; neither shall they need sustenance nor shall they cast a shadow, while the god who will have brought this about shall have quiet and shall rest, not for a long while indeed for a god, but for such time as would be reasonable for a man who falls asleep. Such is the mythology of the Magians."[110]

There are a number of texts by Greek and Persian writers that reflect this battle, for example in addition to those mentioned already, the Persian *Pahlavi* texts states in context of a heretical sect called Zurvanism, an offshoot from Zoroastrianism:

"When nothing existed at all, neither heaven nor earth, the great god Zurvan (Infinite Time) alone existed, whose name means 'fate' or 'fortune'. He offered sacrifice for a thousand years that perchance he might have a son who should be called Ohrmazd (Ahura Mazda or Hormozd) and who would create heaven and earth. At the end of this period of a thousand years he began to ponder and said to himself: "What use is this sacrifice that I am offering, and will I really have a son called Ohrmazd, or am I taking all this trouble in vain?" And no sooner had this thought occurred to him then both Ohrmazd and Ahriman were conceived - Ohrmazd because of the sacrifice he had offered, and Ahriman because of his doubt. When he realized that there were two sons in the womb, he made a vow saying: 'Whichever of the two shall come to me first, him will I make king.' Ohrmazd was apprised of his father's thought and revealed it to Ahriman. When Ahriman heard this, he ripped the womb open, emerged, and advanced towards his father. Zurvan, seeing him, asked him: 'Who art thou?' And he replied: 'I am thy son, Ohrmazd.' And Zurvan said: 'My son is light and fragrant, but thou art dark and stinking.' And he wept most bitterly. And as they were talking together, Ohrmazd was born in his turn, light and fragrant; and Zurvan, seeing him, knew that it was his son Ohrmazd for whom he had offered sacrifice. Taking the barsom twigs he held in his hands with which he had been sacrificing, he gave them to Ohrmazd and said: 'Up till now it is I who

---

110 Plurarch's De Iside et Osiride, Griffiths

have offered thee sacrifice; from now on shalt thou sacrifice to me.' But even as Zurvan handed the sacrificial twigs to Ohrmazd, Ahriman drew near and said to him: 'Didst thou not vow that whichever of the sons should come to thee first, to him wouldst thou give the kingdom?' And Zurvan said to him: 'O false and wicked one, the kingdom shall be granted thee for nine thousand years, but Ohrmazd have I made a king above thee, and after nine thousand years he will reign and will do everything according to his good pleasure.' And Ohrmazd created the heavens and the earth and all things that are beautiful and good; but Ahriman created the demons and all that is evil and perverse. Ohrmazd created riches, Ahriman poverty."[111]

The same polarity is also referred to in Zoroastrian text *Yasna 30.3-4:*

"Truly there are two primal Spirits, twins renowned to be in conflict. In thought and word, in act they are two: the better and the bad. And those who act well have chosen rightly between these two, not so the evil doers. And when these two spirits first came together they created life and not-life, and how at the end Worst Existence shall be for the wicked, but (the House of) Best purpose for the just man."[112]

An example for the role of humanity in this battle can be seen in *Yasht to Tir* (Hymn to the star Sirius), here the Angel star Sirius, the bringer of rain, battles the demon of drought. The people forget to make the appropriate libation and offerings to him, hence he losses the battle with the demon of drought. Sirius then appeals to Ahura Mazda directly, who makes him the offering and gives him the strength to defeat drought:

"18. 'The next ten nights, O Spitama Zarathushtra! the bright and glorious Tishtrya mingles his shape with light, moving in the shape of a white, beautiful horse, with golden ears and a golden caparison. 'Here he calls for people to assemble, here he asks, saying:

---

111 The Dawn and Twilight of Zoroastrianism, Zaehner
112 Tishtar Yasht, Darmesteter

'Who now will offer me the libations with the Haoma and the holy meat? To whom shall I give wealth of horses, a troop of horses, and the purification of his own soul? Now I ought to receive sacrifice and prayer in the material world, by the law of excellent holiness.' Then, O Spitama Zarathushtra! the bright and glorious Tishtrya goes down to the sea Vouru-Kasha in the shape of a white, beautiful horse, with golden ears and a golden caparison. 'But there rushes down to meet him the Daeva Apaosha, in the shape of a dark horse, black with black ears, black with a black back, black with a black tail, stamped with brands of terror. 'They meet together, hoof against hoof, O Spitama Zarathushtra! the bright and glorious Tishtrya and the Daeva Apaosha. They fight together, O Spitama Zarathushtra! for three days and three nights. And then the Daeva Apaosha proves stronger than the bright and glorious Tishtrya, he overcomes him. 'And Tishtrya flees from the sea Vouru-Kasha, as far as a Hathra's length. He cries out in woe and distress, the bright and glorious Tishtrya: 'Woe is me, O Ahura Mazda! I am in distress, O Waters and Plants! O Fate and thou, Law of the worshippers of Mazda! Men do not worship me with a sacrifice in which I am invoked by my own name, as they worship the other Yazatas with sacrifices in which they are invoked by their own names. If men had worshipped me with a sacrifice in which I had been invoked by my own name, as they worship the other Yazatas with sacrifices in which they are invoked by their own names, I should have taken to me the strength of ten horses, the strength of ten camels, the strength of ten bulls, the strength of ten mountains, the strength of ten rivers.' 'Then I, Ahura Mazda, offer up to the bright and glorious Tishtrya a sacrifice in which he is invoked by his own name, and I bring him the strength of ten horses, the strength of ten camels, the strength of ten bulls, the strength of ten mountains, the strength of ten rivers. 'Then, O Spitama Zarathushtra! the bright and glorious Tishtrya goes down to the sea Vouru-Kasha in the shape of a white, beautiful horse, with golden ears and golden caparison. But there rushes down to meet him the Daeva Apaosha in the shape of a dark horse, black with black ears, black with a black back, black with a black tail, stamped with brands of terror. 'They meet together, hoof against hoof, O Spitama Zarathushtra! the bright and glorious Tishtrya, and the Daeva Apaosha; they fight *together, O Zarathushtra! till the time of noon. Then the bright and glorious Tishtrya proves stronger than the Daeva Apaosha, he overcomes him. 'Then he goes from the sea Vouru-Kasha as far as a Hathra's length: 'Hail!' cries the bright and glorious Tishtrya.'Hail unto me, O Ahura Mazda! Hail unto you, O waters and plants! Hail, O Law of the worshippers of Mazda! Hail will it be unto you, O lands! The life of the waters will flow down unrestrained to the big-seeded corn fields, to the small-seeded pasture-fields, and to the whole of the material world!'"[113]*

Another figure that appears in the this cycle is the figure of the demoness Jahi or Jeh the whore, who is the only demon that manages to wake Ahriman from his 3000 years of sleep. In the Zoroastrian text *Bundahishn* the story is written, and she is rewarded for her success in rising Ahriman:

"And, again, the wicked Jeh shouted thus: 'Rise up, thou father of us! for in that conflict I will shed thus much vexation on the righteous man and the labouring ox that, through my deeds, life will not be wanted, and I will destroy their living souls (nismo); I will vex the water, I will vex the plants, I will vex the fire of Ohrmazd, I will make the whole creation of Ohrmazd vexed.' And she so recounted those evil deeds a second time, that the evil spirit was delighted and started up from that confusion; and he kissed Jeh upon the head, and the pollution which they call menstruation became apparent in Jeh. He shouted to Jeh thus: 'What is thy wish? so that I may give it thee.' And Jeh shouted to the evil spirit thus: 'A man is the wish, so give it to me.' The form of the evil spirit was a log-like lizard's (vazak) body, and he appeared a young man of fifteen years to Jeh, and that brought the thoughts of Jeh to him."[114]

The greatest demon created by Ahriman is the Azi Dahâka (the dragon), who is a three headed dragon who later in the book *Shahnameh* (the book of kings) becomes Zahak. Zahak is a evil king with a serpent on each of his shoulders, which he has to be feed with human brains every day. In earlier Zoroastrian

---

113 Tishtar Yasht, Darmesteter
114 Ibid.

versions of the story (*Yasht 19, 50*), Atar, the lord of fire and son of Ahura Mazda attacks the dragon Azi Dahâka. He tells the dragon:

> "There give it up to me thou three-mouthed Azi Dahâka. If thou seizest that Glory that cannot be forcibly seized, then I will enter thy hinder part, I will blaze up in thy jaws, so that thou mayest never more rush upon the earth made by Mazda and destroy the world of the good principle. Then Azi took back his hands, as the instinct of life prevailed, so much had Âtar affrighted him."[115]

The Persian dragon slayer is Thraêtaona who defeats Azi Dahâka by binding him and imprisoning him deep in a mountain top. To achieve this Thraêtaona makes many offerings to the goddess Drvâspa whose name means *'with solid horses'* and is probably linked to the sea goddess Anahita as they both share similar characteristics. It is with the backing of the goddess Drvâspa that Thraêtaona wins against the dragon. In *Yasht 9* we read:

> "To her did Thraêtaona, the heir of the valiant Âthwya clan, offer up a sacrifice in the four-cornered Varena, with a hundred male horses, a thousand oxen, ten thousand lambs, and with an offering of libations: 'Grant me this boon, O good, most beneficent Drvâspa! that I may overcome Azi Dahâka, the three-mouthed, the three-headed, the six-eyed, who has a thousand senses, that most powerful, fiendish Drug, that demon, baleful to the world, the strongest Drug that Angra Mainyu created against the material world, to destroy the world of the good principle; and that I may deliver his two wives, Savanghavâk and Erenavâk, who are the fairest of body amongst women, and the most wonderful creatures in the world. The powerful Drvâspa, made by Mazda, the holy Drvâspa, the maintainer, granted him that boon, as he was offering up libations, giving gifts, sacrificing, and entreating that she would grant him that boon."[116]

The dragon is defeated, but not slain; he is kept captive in the Mount Devamand until the end of the world.

---

115 Ibid.
116 Menog-i Khrad, West, 1885.

There are many more angels and demons in Zoroastrianism than I have mentioned here, there is also class of lesser demons called the Pairakas, who are female and can take many forms, and are akin to the European fairy figures.

In the *Menog-i Khrad* (*'The Spirit of Wisdom'*) text the angels and demons the dead person soul's meet at the Chinvat Bridge are described. The soul of a person is represented as a maiden whose appearance depends on ones deeds:

> *"110. Thou should not become presumptuous through life; for death comes upon thee at last, the dog and the bird lacerate the corpse, and the perishable part (sejinako) falls to the ground. During three days and nights the soul sits at the crown of the head of the body. And the fourth day, in the light of dawn with the cooperation of Sraosha the righteous, Vae the good, and Warharan the strong, the opposition of Astwihad, Vae the bad, Frazishto the demon, and Nizishto the demon, and the evil-designing action of Eshm, the evil-doer, the impetuous assailant it goes up to the awful, lofty Chinvat bridge, to which every one, righteous and wicked, is coming. And many opponents have watched there, with the desire of evil of Eshm, the impetuous assailant, and of Astwihad who devours creatures of every kind and knows no satiety, and the mediation of Sraosha (Obedience), Mithra (Covenant) and Rashnu (Justice) and the weighing of Rashnu, the just, with the balance of the spirits, which renders no favour on any side, neither for the righteous nor yet the wicked, neither for the lords nor yet the monarchs. As much as a hair's breadth it will not turn, and has no partiality; and he who is a lord and monarch it considers equally, in its decision, with him who is the least of mankind."*

> *"And when a soul of the righteous passes upon that bridge, the width of the bridge becomes as it were a league (parasang), and the righteous soul passes over with the cooperation of Sraosha the righteous. And his own deeds of a virtuous kind come to meet him in the form of a maiden, who is handsomer and better than every maiden in the world. If the person had performed evil deeds then the reverse occurs at the Chinvat Bridge; Vizaresh, the demon, drags the person to the inevitable House of Lies (hell) and the person is greeted by a vile and*

hideous maiden who is the manifestation of their bad deeds."

It is easy to see why Zoroastrianism is seen as the prototype to much of Judaism, Christianity and Islam, which led the scholar Mary Boyce to state:

"Zoroaster was thus the first to teach the doctrines of an individual judgment, Heaven and Hell, the future resurrection of the body, the general Last Judgment, and life everlasting for the reunited soul and body. These doctrines were to become familiar articles of faith to much of mankind, through borrowings by Judaism, Christianity and Islam; yet it is in Zoroastrianism itself that they have their fullest logical coherence....." [117]

The meaning of the Faravahar or the Holy Guardian Angel

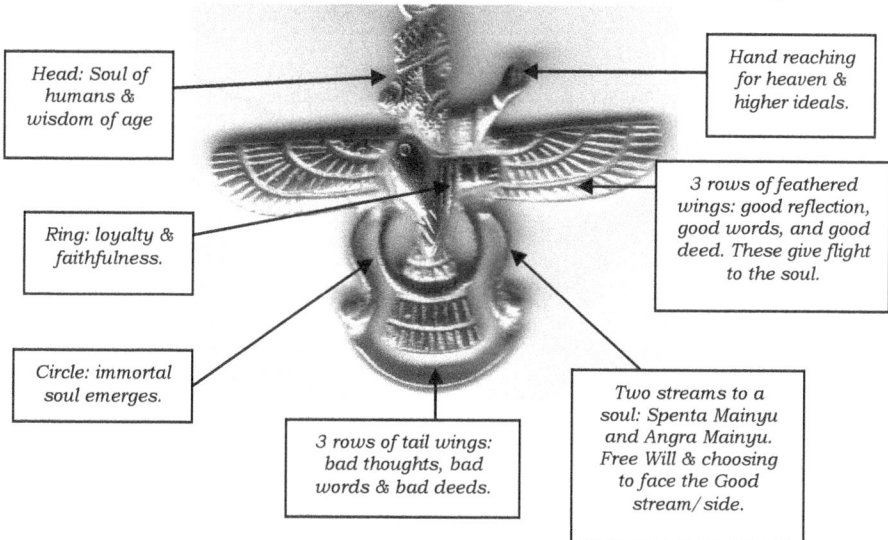

Head: Soul of humans & wisdom of age

Hand reaching for heaven & higher ideals.

3 rows of feathered wings: good reflection, good words, and good deed. These give flight to the soul.

Ring: loyalty & faithfulness.

Circle: immortal soul emerges.

3 rows of tail wings: bad thoughts, bad words & bad deeds.

Two streams to a soul: Spenta Mainyu and Angra Mainyu. Free Will & choosing to face the Good stream/side.

---

117 Zoroastrians: Their Religious Beliefs and Practices, Boyce, 1979.

Acknowledgements:
I would like to thank Katherine Sutherland, Parviz Varjavand, Dina G McIntyre and Zaneta Garratt for their helpful comments.

Bibliography
Boyce, Mary; *Textual Sources for the Study of Zoroastrianism*; 1990; University of Chicago Press; Chicago

Clark, Peter; *Zoroastrianism: An Introduction to an Ancient Faith*; 1998; Sussex Academic Press; Sussex

Cotterell, Arthur; *The Ultimate Encyclopaedia of Mythology*; 2003; Hermes House; London

Darmesteter, James (trans); *Avesta Khorda Avesta* (Book of Common Prayer); Sacred Books of the East, volume 3; 1898; USA

Eliade, Mircea; *A History of Religious Ideas: Vol 1 From the Stone Age to the Eleusinian Mysteries*; 1978; Collins; London

King, Charles William (trans); *Plutarch's Morals: Theosophical Essays On Isis and Osiris*; 1908

West, E.W. (trans); *The Bundahishn (Creation), or Knowledge from the Zand*; 1897; Sacred Books of the East, volume 5; Oxford University Press; Oxford

Zaehner, R.C.; *The Dawn and Twilight of Zoroastrianism*; 1961; G.P. Putnams Sons; New York

MITHRAS, SLAYING A BULL (FROM THE BOOK 'BRITISH MUSEUM', SIR HENRY ELLIS, 1836)

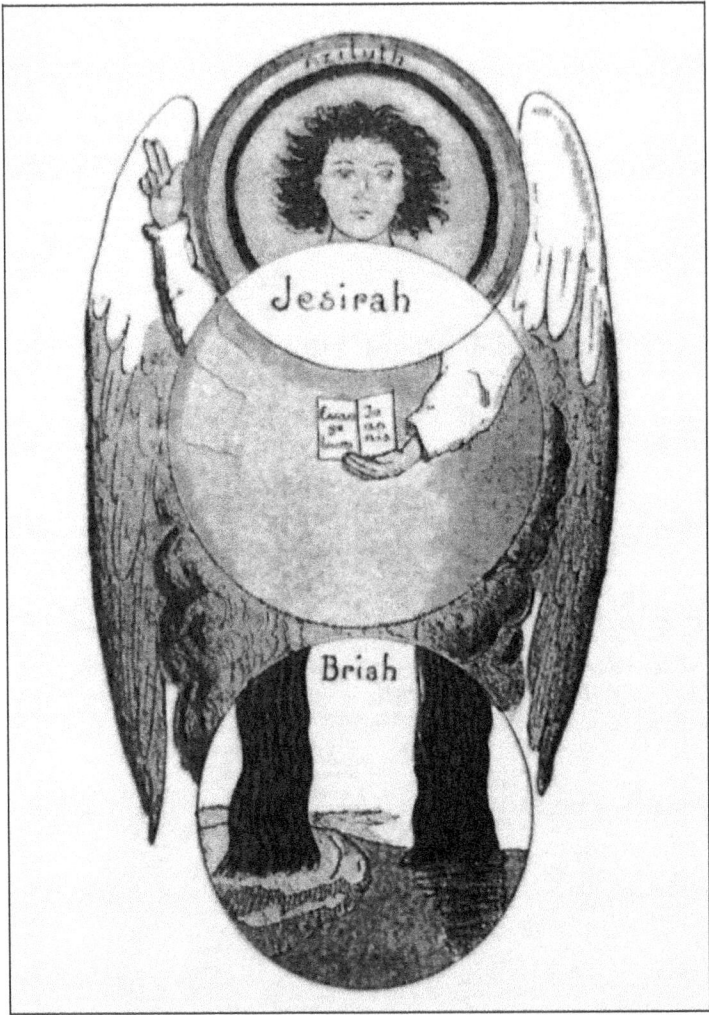

THE INSPIRING ANGEL OF ELIPHAS LEVI'S "THE MYSTERIES OF THE QABALAH"

REPRESENTING THE UNION OF THE FOUR WORLDS.

INDEX

Printed in May 2024
by Rotomail Italia S.p.A., Vignate (MI) - Italy